MASTER STROKES

MASTER STROKES

401 Proven Lessons for Mastering Every Golf Shot

by Nick Mastroni and Phil Franké

RUNNING PRESS
PHILADELPHIA · LONDON

9   8   7   6   5   4   3   2   1
Digit on the right indicates the number of this printing

Library of Congress Control Number 20002096412

ISBN 0-7624-1581-9

Cover and Interior designed by Matt Goodman
Edited by Greg Jones
Typography: Franklin Gothic and Rubino

This book may be ordered by mail from the publisher.
Please include $2.50 for postage and handling.
But try your bookstore first!

Running Press Book Publishers
125 South Twenty-second Street
Philadelphia, Pennsylvania 19103-4399

Visit us on the web!
www.runningpress.com

TABLE OF CONTENTS

INTRODUCTION

Master Strokes is quite likely the most complete compilation of golf instruction ever presented as a single publication. It was not actually our initial intent to assemble such a daunting collection. The lessons you will read and hopefully enjoy and learn from, have been appearing individually as a syndicated newspaper column under the title of Master Strokes, since March 1999. As these columns have circulated, we began receiving frequent inquiries as to whether the lessons existed in book form. We have had to reply that unfortunately they did not—until now.

Inside you will find a total of 401 bite-sized, fully illustrated lessons covering nearly every playing situation that may occur from the moment you lace up your spikes until you replace the flag on the 18th green. In fact, there are even some tips on what to do before you step on the course to better your conditioning, and therefore your game.

The lessons are divided into 15 sections, beginning with pre-round preparation, going through the full swing and the various other areas of play, and ending with instruction on rules and etiquette. As you read the swing and shot instruction in particular, keep this in mind: You should not try to incorporate the information in every lesson into your game. There are three good reasons:

1. You will find that certain swing problems will be discussed, with opposing corrections provided. That's because different players have flaws that straddle both sides of a happy medium. For example, one player's swing plane might be too flat, with the club moving too much in a horizontal fashion, while another's might be too upright, that is, moving too much on a vertical plane. You need only concern yourself with the lesson that applies to your particular side of the problem.

2. Different golfers will have different problem areas. For example, you may be getting excellent results with your full swing, but your short game is substandard and your putting only fair at best. Certainly, go right to the short game and putting sections. There is no requirement to read Master Strokes from cover to cover, and/or in the order in which the lessons appear.

3. You may occasionally note that the same area of instruction is discussed in more than one lesson. This is particularly true in Section 3, The Full Swing. Sometimes, two golfers who struggle with the same swing flaw will respond differently to two different images that are intended to solve the same problem. You get to decide in these cases which lesson "clicks" best for you.

Finally, after you read these lessons, please give yourself time to ingrain the instruction into your game. Even the most beneficial adjustment may cause you problems at first, based solely on the fact that you are unfamiliar with it. Don't try to change too many things too quickly. If you take a patient approach, the information in Master Strokes will help you play better for many years to come. The goal is to improve your game, one stroke at a time.

PREPARING TO PLAY

The vast majority of amateur golfers put themselves at a terrible disadvantage before they ever tee off. How? By the very fact that they have done nothing to prepare either their bodies or their minds for the upcoming round. There isn't a professional in the world who would feel capable of rushing to the first tee without any pre-round preparation, and then play his or her best. If that's true for the pros, why should it be any different for you?

This brief introductory section will provide you with a number of useful ways to prepare for your round so that you can get the very most out of your skills.

PREPARING TO PLAY

MASTER·STROKES

Stretch Before You Swing

While you may think you can get away with running to the first tee with no warm-up, a pre-round stretching routine is a must not only to swing the club your best but to maintain your health. Always spend 5-10 minutes on a stretching routine either at home or at the course, focusing particularly on loosening your lower back, the area most prone to injury. Only after this stretching should you hit 15-20 easy warm-up shots on the practice tee, and only then should you tee off.

The result will be not only a freer swing and better play but a greatly lessened chance of injury as well.

MASTER·STROKES

Get Your Lower Back Limber

When your lower back is stiff, your play will suffer because you won't turn well enough to generate much force.
If you don't stretch anything else, at the very least, stretch your lower back before every round. Do this with the help of a golf cart: Stand to the side of the cart, bend your knees slightly and grasp either the seat handle or a roof support with both hands. Then sit back as far as you can while keeping your arms extended. Hold this stretch for 15 seconds, then repeat. You'll immediately feel the difference.

MASTER STROKES

Get To Course Early

It's never a good idea to get to the course just before your tee time, so that you rush onto the first tee without even a practice swing.

You'll greatly improve your enjoyment and your score if you make it a rule to get to the course at least 30 minutes before your scheduled start. This will allow you to do five minutes of stretching exercises; then hit some easy practice shots for 15 minutes (20-25 balls); and finally, to spend 10 minutes getting a feel for your putting stroke and hitting a few chips. You'll head to the first tee loose, confident and ready to go.

MASTER·STROKES

Warm Up!

Ever play a round where your score is ruined before you've finished the first few holes? You'll greatly reduce the chance of this if you'll simply commit to a brief warm-up session before every round.

Your goal in a warmup is not to perfect your swing. It's simply to loosen your muscles, get the feel of the clubface on the ball, and observe any particular flight pattern to your shots. Even if you only hit 15 balls — three balls each with every third club — you'll have an awareness of what to expect that can help you get off to a good start.

MASTER·STROKES

Stretch The Left Shoulder

An area that receives a lot of stress in the golf swing, and needs to be kept supple and loose, is the left shoulder. It's particularly important to keep it stretched prior to starting play. Here's a simple way to do it: Take your left arm and extend it across your chest. Hook your right forearm in front of your left triceps. Slowly pull the left arm in as far as you can, feeling the stretch in the deltoid muscle. Hold for 15 seconds, rest, then repeat the exercise. This stretch reduces the chance of injury to this key area during the round.

MASTER·STROKES

Be "Prepped" To Play

Ever play golf with somebody who rushes to the first tee, then is constantly searching for things during play? It can be aggravating. It's good etiquette to have everything you need, where you need it. Before you get to the first tee, put non-golf items (keys, wallet, handkerchief) in a single pants pocket or your golf bag. Then have one pocket where you keep the following: 8-10 golf tees; several small coins (pennies, dimes) to mark your ball with; a greens-repair tool for fixing ball marks (it is also good to clean your spikes with; and an extra ball in case you need a provisional. Finally, always have a towel attached to your golf bag. Being organized helps speed play and will help your game, too.

MASTER·STROKES

The 10-Minute Warmup

You've heard the advice to get to the course early for a thorough pre-round preparation. But, things happen, and you've arrived only 10 minutes before tee-off. How can you get the most out of those 10 minutes? Do the following:

1. Go to the practice tee and stretch your lower back (2 minutes).

2. Hit just 6-10 balls, without rushing. Hit half with an easy pitching wedge, half with a middle iron (3 minutes).

3. Go to the edge of the practice green and hit several chip shots (2 minutes).

4. Hit three or four long putts to different targets; just before you go to the tee, hit a few straight, uphill 3-foot putts to boost your confidence (3 minutes).

You're up!

MASTER STROKES

Loosen Your Lower Back

A supple lower back will greatly aid both your swing and your enjoyment of the game.

So, make it a habit to do some stretching exercises for your lower back before you go to the course. A good one is as follows: Lie on your back with your knees bent. Pull one knee in to your chest. Hold it there for five seconds as you feel the stretch in your lower back. Then pull your opposite knee into your chest and hold for a count of five. Repeat the exercise 10 times on each side. Your lower back will feel more limber as soon as you get up from the floor!

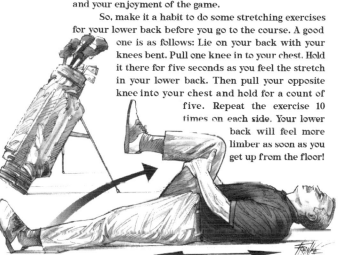

MASTER·STROKES

100
80
60
40
20

Less warmup

More warmup

Adjust Your Warmups

Most golfers understand that a brief stretching and warmup routine will help them get the round off to a good start. When it's cold and/or windy, allow more time for your warmup. Do two or three extra minutes of stretching before going to the practice tee. Once there, hit 10 extra balls in leisurely fashion, say 30 instead of 20, keeping it simple and focusing on a slow, rhythmic tempo. On the other hand, when it's very hot, your body will be looser and fatigue may become a factor late in the round. So it's a good idea to hit just 15 or so shots prior to teeing off. Finally, make sure to drink plenty of water before and during play.

MASTER·STROKES

Forward Tees
In Winter Weather

In the off-season, it's harder to shoot good scores. In cold weather the ball won't fly as far, and course conditions are not as lush. You can easily shoot three to five shots higher than normal, and start losing confidence. A suggestion: During winter, tee off from forward tees, so the course is, say, 400 to 500 yards shorter. This will more than offset the fact that your shots are flying a little shorter. Also, it's good to play shots into greens with different clubs than you're used to, as will be the case when you tee off from farther forward. This keeps your thinking fresh. And, a few low scores over the winter will boost your confidence for the coming season!

HOLE 8
YARDS ~~424~~ 378
PAR 4

MASTER·STROKES

Overcoming First-Tee Jitters

Many amateurs get nervous before their opening tee shot, particularly when there are a number of onlookers. The tendency is to give yourself negative advice such as, "Don't top it," and to place too much importance on the shot as a "mood setter" for the round. With all this pressure, you're not likely to make a very good swing.

Two tips for overcoming the jitters: **1.** Remember that your first shot is no more or less important than any stroke you'll play (including a two-foot putt you might have in a few minutes). No one shot will make or break a round. **2.** Stay in your pre-shot routine, which should always be brief and decisive, then immediately move into the swing without any hesitation.

Section 2:

PRE-SWING FUNDMENTALS

Before you draw the club away from the ball, there are a number of pre-swing or "setup" fundamentals to be aware of. These pre-swing fundamentals for the most part can be divided into four categories: Grip, Stance, Posture, and Alignment. A player who is sound in these four areas will have a much greater chance of producing a high-quality swing than will the golfer who is not. In addition to providing advice on all of these areas, this section also includes tips on several other steps that must take place before you commence the swing.

CONTENTS

MASTER·STROKES

Take the Stance Of An Athlete

Generating high clubhead speed and hitting the ball squarely is harder than you may think. One "must" for fine shots is good balance. Set up in a posture like that of athletes in other sports who are in perfect balance. Your knees should have a nice flex with your weight on the ball of each foot. Your stance should be shoulder-width with the driver. Your back should be angled slightly forward and straight with your chin slightly up, your arms hanging lightly with no tension.

Starting from the athletic position described makes it much easier to swing the club while maintaining perfect balance—the secret to consistent shotmaking.

MASTER·STROKES

Grip A "Square" Handle

Here's how to put your hands in a good gripping position: Imagine that the grip is square rather than round. Assume your left-hand grip, placing your left thumb on the top-right corner of the grip. When you put your right hand on the club, your right thumb should rest on the top-left corner. The right palm will fit nicely over the left thumb so that the hands feel like a unit. This positioning should remain constant, regardless of whether you use an "interlocking" or "overlapping" grip.

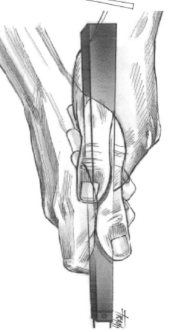

MASTER·STROKES

Find Your Ball Position

Many golfers are confused about where to position the ball in their stance. Here's a sure way to find the right spot: Go to a soft field with an iron club. Take your normal setup, then swing so you take a noticeable divot. Note where the divot lies in relation to your feet. For short and middle irons, play the ball one inch behind where the divot starts, so you make contact while the club is still descending. For long irons and fairway woods, play it one ball-width more forward, so you make contact at nearly the bottom of the swing. With a teed-up driver, move it one ball-width more forward, so you connect as the club is just beginning to ascend from its lowest point.

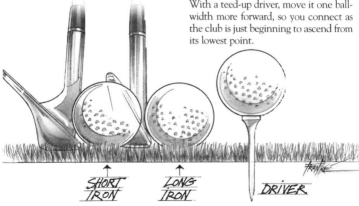

SHORT IRON   LONG IRON   DRIVER

MASTER·STROKES

Bend From The Waist

Quite a few amateurs make an error in their posture at address. The back is too upright, which can cause two problems: 1. It leads to a swing that's too flat, too much around the body; 2. It encourages the player to reach unnaturally with the arms, which adds tension and makes a perfect return of the clubhead at impact difficult.

Practice setting up in front of a mirror with your knees slightly flexed, and with your back bent forward from the waist but straight. From this position, you can let your arms hang in a natural and relaxed position, yet they'll have plenty of room to clear your body during the swing.

MASTER·STROKES

Align "Parallel Left"

Quite a few amateurs commit an error when setting up to the ball that's easy to make. They line up with their bodies aimed directly at the target. While this sounds correct, in actuality, your shoulders, hips, knees and feet should ideally point "parallel left" of the target. This means a line across these body parts should be parallel to a line that runs directly from your ball to the target. Such an alignment, even if it feels slightly left, will allow you to swing the clubhead naturally along the target line and start the ball on-target.

MASTER·STROKES

Grip Across Left-Hand Fingers

If you are looking for a little more power, the answer may literally rest in the palm of your hand. Or more accurately, in your fingers.

Many golfers grip the club in the palm of the left hand, in too much of a "fisty" manner. This limits the leverage they can generate through the unhinging of the left wrist through impact. When you begin to assemble your grip, make sure the handle lies atop the fingers of your left hand at a slight diagonal, rather than in the palm. Then simply close your hand over the grip. With the club held in the fingers, it will be much easier to uncock your wrists actively through the impact zone, fully utilizing this "power lever" in the swing.

MASTER·STROKES

Set Clubface First

Many amateurs align both their bodies and the clubface poorly in relation to the target. Then, even if they make a fine swing, the shot goes off-line.

Here's a tip that will help you get both the club and your body aligned on-target. As you're stepping up to the shot, but before you take your stance, carefully align the leading edge of the clubface toward your target. Then, without moving the clubhead, set your feet and the rest of your body at right angles to that leading edge. This simple setup habit will add accuracy to your shots.

Step in

1

2

MASTER·STROKES

Is Upper Body Square To Target?

You've probably heard that on full shots, you should align yourself so that a line across the toes is parallel to your target line. While this is good advice, it's not the whole story. Your entire body should align parallel to the target line. In fact, it's more important that your shoulders be square to the target, because their alignment will control the path of the swing. It's possible to align your feet squarely but to misalign your shoulders. Most often the error will be that they are open, or aiming left.

On the practice tee, ask a friend to check your shoulder alignment by holding a club across them. Keep your upper body square, and you'll find it's much easier to start your shots on-target.

MASTER·STROKES

Strengthen Your Grip

Most golfers who don't hit the ball as far as they'd like will benefit from playing most of their shots with a right-to-left draw. This type of shot provides additional roll and helps fight windy conditions.

If you're having trouble drawing the ball, consider "strengthening" your grip. This means you should turn both hands slightly farther to the right on the club's handle. Your check point: When viewed from the front, the creases between the thumb and forefingers of both hands should point to 11 o'clock on an imaginary clock face.

MASTER·STROKES

55% _driver_ **45%**

for the type of shot you are playing. For a teed-up driver, put slightly more weight on your right foot than your left (55% to 45%). This will help you stay slightly "behind" the ball so you sweep it away at impact. For a normal short-iron shot (7-, 8-, 9-, wedge), you want to make a descending blow that adds backspin and "stop" to the shot. Here, address with 60% of your weight on your left foot, 40% right.

Correct Weight Distributions

In order to make a well-balanced swing, you should start with your weight fairly evenly distributed between the feet (as well as evenly distributed from heel to toe). However, keep in mind that slight adjustments in weight distribution at address will "prep" you for the most desirable impact position

40% _short iron_ **60%**

MASTER·STROKES

30° toward target

Turn Left Toe Out

Less-supple golfers should do all they can to generate a full and free weight shift and body turn through the impact zone. Here's a simple aid to doing this: At address, angle your left toe out about 30 degrees, instead of setting it perpendicular to the target line. This small adjustment in effect gives your left leg and hip more freedom to turn counterclockwise through impact, whereas keeping your left foot perpendicular to the target line hinders this free movement.

Moving your lower-body weight fully and freely through impact will add height and length to your full shots. So keep the left foot angled out.

MASTER·STROKES

Line Up The Leading Edge

It does no good to strike an iron shot solidly, but hit it off-line so that it finds a bunker or otherwise misses the green. However, many golfers have difficulty lining up the clubface to the target, particularly with the shorter irons. This is because they tend to look at the more rounded top line of the clubhead when they address the ball.

Instead, carefully align the straight leading edge of the clubface to your target as you begin your setup. Set this leading edge square to your target, then step into your stance by placing your body at perfect right angles to the leading edge. More on-line approach shots will be the result.

MASTER·STROKES

Setup Basics
For Solid Iron Play

You'll rarely see a golfer hit consistently good irons if their setup is poor. Here are the keys to good setup and posture: **1.** Align clubface squarely to the target, with shoulders, hips, knees and feet perfectly parallel to your target line. **2.** Position ball slightly ahead of stance center, with your hands set 1 to 2 inches ahead of the ball. This sets you up to deliver a slightly descending blow that adds backspin and control. **3.** Develop a balanced and athletic posture, arms hanging naturally rather than reaching, with weight between the balls and heels of the feet. You're in position to make a good turn without any extraneous movement, and deliver the clubface squarely at impact.

MASTER·STROKES

Overlap Vs. Interlock Grip

The most-used grip in golf is called the "overlap", popularized by British golf great Harry Vardon. In this grip for the right-handed player, the right little finger rests between or overlaps the first and second fingers of the left hand. This overlapping helps mesh the hands together.

An alternative is the interlock grip. Here, the right little finger locks in underneath the index finger of the left hand, if anything making a tighter connection between the hands. It's considered helpful for golfers with smaller hands. Although fewer players employ the interlock grip, two of golf's greatest—Jack Nicklaus and Tiger Woods— do so.

Overlap

VS

Interlock

MASTER·STROKES

Don't Reach At Address

More amateurs stand too far from the ball at address than too close to it. This is particularly true with the long clubs. If your arms are stretched taut so that they are almost on the same line as the shaft of your driver, it's a sure sign you are reaching too far and have too much tension in your forearms.

At address, keep your arms relaxed, with your forearms hanging almost straight down and no more than six inches from your body. From a side view, you should see a definite angle between your forearms and the clubshaft, rather than a straight line.

6"

MASTER·STROKES

Move Ball Up In Stance

Golfers who generate a little less clubhead speed than in the past will benefit from playing the ball a touch more forward in relation to the feet. This is particularly true for iron shots. If you position the ball at the center of your stance, you'll hit down on the shot with your hands well ahead. This de-lofts the club; unless you generate lots of clubhead speed, your shots will fly too low. Also, hitting down means more stress on your joints.

If you've been having trouble with low iron shots, try moving the ball forward in your stance, nearly opposite your left heel. This allows you to make contact at the bottom of the swing, so that you utilize all of the club's loft.

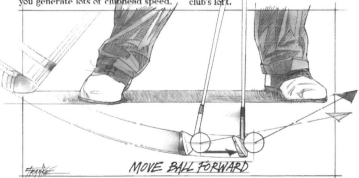

MOVE BALL FORWARD

MASTER·STROKES

Adjust Body, Not Clubface

Many golfers who attempt to draw a shot from right-to-left, or fade it from left-to-right, make a basic error in setting up. They aim both their bodies and the clubface to the side they want the ball to start on. Result: The desired draw or fade doesn't come off.

For any shot (straight shot, draw or fade), always align the leading edge directly at your target. Then adjust your body alignment: For a draw, align shoulders, hips, knees and feet slightly right of the target line. For a fade, align these body parts slightly left. When you make your normal swing from these altered body positions, the clubhead will move into the ball from slightly across the target line. This altered path combined with the square clubface will supply the desired sidespin to the shot.

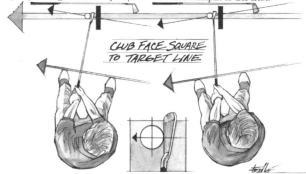

CLUB FACE SQUARE
TO TARGET LINE

MASTER·STROKES

Left Thumb On Right Side

If the left hand does not support the club well, it will cause the clubhead to slow before impact, and contact will feel "dead." So, it's important that the left hand be positioned correctly to withstand the force of impact. As you close your left hand around the club, make sure that the middle of your left thumb is well to the right of the top-center of the shaft, rather than right on the top.

Test by hitting one-handed chip shots with your left thumb placed on the right side of the grip, then by hitting some with your left thumb on top. The difference in the feel at impact will convince you that you'll get a much more solid feel — and more speed - by moving your left thumb to the right.

MASTER·STROKES

Rotate Head To Right

While every golfer would like to make a nice full shoulder turn on the backswing, this is difficult for some less-flexible golfers to accomplish. A good tip: Just before you take the clubhead away, rotate your head slightly to

the right, so that you're looking at the ball primarily out of your left eye. By doing this, your upper spine and your chin are already pre-set to the right in relation to the ball's position. This in turn means you will be able to turn your shoulders a little farther than you could if you started the swing with your chin pointed at the ball.

MASTER·STROKES

Tee Ball Higher With Driver

If your swing speed is down a bit from in years past, and your tee shots aren't carrying as far as you'd like, try this: With the driver, tee your ball about one-quarter inch higher than normal. You should see two-thirds of the ball above the clubface at address, rather than one-half as is often recommended. With the ball teed high and a normal swing, more of the clubhead's mass will be below the equator of the ball at impact. This means that the driver will launch the ball at a higher angle than normal, which is necessary with a slightly slower swing speed to give your tee shots their maximum carry.

MASTER·STROKES

Consider the 10-Finger Grip

Older players who may have developed some arthritis in the fingers, may find that the more conventional "overlap" or "interlock" grips cause pain or discomfort. If this is the case, there's nothing wrong with trying the "10-finger" grip. Here, all four fingers of the right hand are directly on the club's handle. You may find this type of hold to be more comfortable. Also, if you tend to slice, the 10-finger grip allows the right hand a more dominant role, which in turn allows you to more easily square the clubface at impact.

MASTER·STROKES

Foward Press

OR

Knee Kick

Develop A Swing Trigger

It's much easier to get the swing off to a smooth, rhythmic start if you develop a specific motion or "swing trigger," rather than starting from a dead standstill. There is no one correct swing trigger, but many that are helpful. You may want to use a slight forward press, in which you push your hands an inch or two toward the target before letting them recoil into the takeaway. You might try a forward press of the right knee, in which you kick in that knee toward the target before starting back. Or, you may hold the club very lightly, then firm up your grip pressure just slightly as a cue to draw the club back. Practice one of these swing triggers and see which one helps you get the smoothest start.

MASTER·STROKES

Pick A Tiny Target

You'll focus the best on the tee shot at hand if you make it a habit to pick out the smallest target possible to aim at. Don't simply think in terms of hitting the fairway or even one side of the fairway. Instead, pick out some specific, visible point as your target. Usually, this specific point will be something in the distance rather than part of the fairway itself. Aim for a particular branch on a tree, or the top of a church steeple, or perhaps even the flagstick itself. Once you've selected this specific target, keep it in your mind's eye as you finalize your preparation and start your swing.

MASTER STROKES

Cover the Left Thumb

Many amateurs have the following fault in their grips: For right-handers, the right hand is too low on the handle in relation to their left. It appears to be "split" or separated from it. This allows the right hand to overpower the left through the impact zone, causing the clubhead to "flip" through impact with erratic shot results.

A grip key: Whether you use an interlock or overlap style grip, make sure to fold your right palm over the base of your left thumb, so the hands are unitized rather than separated. A helpful key is that as you look down, you should just be able to see the seam on your golf glove at the top of your left thumb, rather than the entire left thumb.

MASTER·STROKES

Elbows In At Address

A good address position tip for amateurs: Set up with your elbows close to your sides at address. Your elbows should be soft and relaxed, rather than stretched away from the body. Prior to the start of the backswing, the elbows should be just touching your sides above the hips. As you start the club back, you should continue to feel your right elbow just barely touching your side.

By keeping your elbows tucked in toward your sides, you encourage a turn of the body to execute the backswing, rather than just swinging your arms while your body is passive. Such a backswing turn helps the club revolve around the body as it should, while at the same time building maximum power.

MASTER·STROKES

A Helpful Flex Check

Many amateurs hurt their chances for good shotmaking because of poor posture at address. They're either too stiff in the legs, making it hard to get down to the ball at impact, or they bend the knees too much so their weight is back on their heels. Here's a tip to help your posture: Have a friend check your address position from behind the target line. You should flex your knees just enough so that a line drawn from your rear end falls just outside the back of your heels. If the line falls well behind the back of your heels, reduce your knee flex, if it falls at or in front of your heels, adjust your posture by flexing your knees a little more.

JUST BACK OF HEELS

Franke

MASTER·STROKES

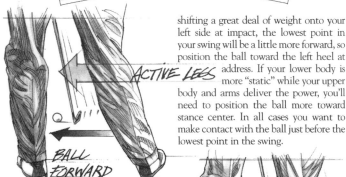

BALL FORWARD

ACTIVE LEGS

shifting a great deal of weight onto your left side at impact, the lowest point in your swing will be a little more forward, so position the ball toward the left heel at address. If your lower body is more "static" while your upper body and arms deliver the power, you'll need to position the ball more toward stance center. In all cases you want to make contact with the ball just before the lowest point in the swing.

Ball Position Varies With Swing Type

Where should you position the ball in your stance? It should not necessarily be the same spot for every player.

For all regular full shots, the ball position is between a line opposite the left heel and a line opposite the center of the stance. If your lower body is active,

STATIC LEGS

BALL BACK

MASTER STROKES

Basics For a Good Grip

There are three elements that should be a part of any good grip: **1.** The club should rest primarily in the fingers, rather than the palms, as this allows the wrists to work freely and add power to the swing. **2.** The hands should be knitted together so that they work as a single unit during the swing. You "knit" the hands together by hooking the right little finger above the left index finger (overlap grip) or underneath it (interlock grip). **3.** Both hands should be placed in the way that makes it easiest to return the clubface squarely to the target at impact. This varies from player to player. You can experiment by moving both hands either more to the right or left on the grip, and observing the differences in ball flight.

MASTER·STROKES

Three Ways To Stop Shanking

Golf's most feared fault is the shanked iron. This happens when the club's hosel meets the ball, so that the ball squirts far right of the target.

Three tips to stop shanking are as follows:

1. Stand one inch farther from the ball, and make sure your arms are comfortably away from your body at address.

2. Put your weight more toward your toes at address so that if anything, you'll "sit back" a bit through impact, helping insure the hosel doesn't strike the ball.

3. Focus your eyes on the nearest or "inside" part of the ball, and aim to swing the clubhead through this spot.

MASTER STROKES

excessive and reflects the player's anxiety over the upcoming shot.

If you're taking lots of waggles, do this: Train yourself to take no more than two waggles once you've set up. On the practice tee, commit to taking either one or two waggles, then starting the backswing immediately from there. Gradually, you'll find yourself playing shots with less anxiety and more confidence.

How Many Waggles?

Most players, after setting up to the ball, "waggle" the club with their hands and wrists prior to starting the swing. It's okay to include a waggle as part of your pre-shot routine. However, some players waggle the club ten or more times before taking it back. This is

Go!

MASTER·STROKES

Interlock Grip
For Shorter Fingers

The most commonly-used grip is the overlap grip, in which the little finger of the right hand overlaps behind the index finger of the left hand. This is fine, except that if your fingers are short, it's harder for the left little finger to stay in it's "overlapped" position—it may pull away at or after impact. So, if your fingers are short, consider the "interlock" grip. This inserts your right little finger underneath the left index finger, knitting the fingers together a bit more securely.

Before you decide to switch to the interlock grip, use it on the practice tee to get the feel of it. Also, any grip change might cause some slight changes in your ball flight, so practice to make sure you know what to expect out on the course.

MASTER·STROKES

Don't "Ground" The Driver

On shots from the tee in particular, you want to take the club away in a smooth, level motion. You'll find it easier to do this if you hover the driver clubhead about a half-inch above the ground, rather than resting it on the turf. When you don't ground the clubhead, there's less of a tendency to pick the club up, as opposed to pushing it back low. Also, when you don't ground the club there's no chance that you'll catch the clubhead on any irregularity in the turf as you draw the club back. So, keep the clubhead just off the ground, and you'll get your swing off to a consistently smooth start.

THE FULL SWING

The perfect golf swing has never been and never will be achieved. The idiosyncrasies of every individual human body make attainment of this Holy Grail impossible. That, however, has never stopped ardent golfers from trying. And, of course, the closer a player can come to perfecting the full swing, the better a player he or she will become.

This section explores all areas of the swing movement, from takeaway to completion of the backswing to the transition into the downswing, on through impact and the follow through. Keep in mind when studying this section, that there are many more tips here than any one player can apply successfully to his or her swing. You will benefit most from this section by taking stock of the current state of your own particular swing movement, understanding what area or areas of your swing need work, and applying the lessons that are pertinent to those areas.

CONTENTS

MASTER·STROKES

Put the Clubhead in the Mitt

Many amateurs drag the clubhead back from the ball too far inside the target line, particularly with the driver. Here's a great image that will help: Imagine a baseball catcher is holding a mitt three feet directly behind you, at knee height. Starting back, simply try to put the clubhead right into the catcher's mitt. By using this image, you'll keep the clubhead much closer to the target line for a longer period in the backswing.

This in turn gives you a nice wide arc for power along with a much better chance to return the club-head to the ball on a path along or slightly inside the target line. Result: More solid, powerful shots.

MASTER STROKES

A Compact Backswing Is Okay

Many golfers assume that a full swing is one in which the clubshaft reaches a position parallel to the ground at the completion of the backswing. This is inaccurate and can be especially harmful to seniors, who may have lost some flexibility.

There is no such thing as a "perfect" length of backswing. Your length of backswing should be the maximum you can make while turning your body fully, staying in balance and maintaining control of the club. If you do these things and your clubshaft comes up short of parallel, that's fine—you will still hit excellent shots and get ample distance even with a slightly shorter backswing.

The Full Swing

MASTER·STROKES

Point Left Elbow Down On Backswing

Most golfers swing the club on too flat a plane, that is, too much around and not enough "up and down." It's hard to hit consistently straight shots this way. A more upright swing plane, where the clubhead stays more "in front" of you, keeps the clubhead moving along the target line longer, greatly aiding accuracy.

To keep your backswing upright, during your next practice session, concentrate on keeping your left (or forward) elbow pointing toward the ground, rather than pointing outward. You'll be pleasantly surprised at how straight your shots fly.

MASTER·STROKES

Maintain Spine Angle

How many times have you topped a shot and heard, "You lifted your head!" When the clubface returns slightly above the ground at impact, raising your spine angle is the real culprit. It happens often when the player takes a big backswing to maximize distance. To stop topping the ball, visualize your spine angled slightly forward at address, and be conscious of rotating around it on the backswing. Swing smoothly, don't try to overpower your shots, and you'll easily get the feel of this circular turn.

MASTER·STROKES

The Left Arm Is Not A Ramrod

You may have often heard the advice, "Keep the left arm straight on the backswing." Generally this is a good idea, as bending your left arm sharply can cause control problems. However, golfers who try to keep the left arm ramrod-straight do themselves more harm than good. Keeping the left arm stiff makes the muscles of your entire left side tight and tense, which inhibits the speed you can swing down with and may also disrupt your overall swing rhythm. So instead of a ramrod-like left arm, keep the arm relaxed and allow it to "give" just a little at the top of the backswing.

MASTER·STROKES

Get A Toe Up On A Good Weight Shift

Many amateurs swing the club with their arms only. You need to make a good active shift of your body weight to your right side on the backswing, then back to your left side on the downswing, to get power into your shots. And a good weight shift starts from the feet up.

On the backswing, shift your weight actively onto your right foot. Don't stay flat-footed; instead, allow your left foot to turn inward toward your right; it's fine to even let your weight shift pull your left heel off the ground as you reach the top of the backswing. Remember, too much weight shift is better than none at all.

MASTER·STROKES

Low, Slow Takeaway

For all regular full shots, but especially those played from the tee, you should start the club back as low and as slowly as possible. As a guideline, try to push the club back low to the ground and very slowly to the point where you see your hands pass over your right foot. If the movement to this point feels ridiculously slow, that's fine. This takeaway allows you to build a full extension of the arms and club on the backswing, which translates to greater power; and it gives you more time to get your body turning on the backswing, rather than making a quicker, handsier, and more inconsistent swing. See if the low, slow takeaway doesn't help your full shots.

MASTER·STROKES

Match Clubface To Left Arm

Watch a good player swing the driver to the top. Note how the clubface lies along the same angle or plane as that formed by the left arm. When the clubface is in this position, there's no need to either consciously or unconsciously manipulate it into a square position at impact. If the clubface points to the sky, however, you'll fight a hook; if it points horizontally, you'll be prone to slicing.

Ask a friend how your driver clubface "hangs," and train yourself to position the clubface so it matches the angle of your left arm. Then you can release freely on the downswing, confident that the clubface will be square at impact.

MASTER·STROKES

Turn The Torso

Many golfers gradually make more and more of an "arm" swing, keeping their torsos relatively stationary while relying on their arms and hands to move the clubhead. Loss of distance is the obvious result.

To get the most out of your swing, you must turn your torso actively on the backswing. The more you can turn your torso away from the target on the backswing, the more naturally it will snap back on the downswing. This is crucial for developing power. Try to make your backswing all "torso turn" and no "arms," rather than vice versa. It may feel funny at first, but when you get back to making a torso turn rather than an arm swing, much stronger shots will result.

MASTER·STROKES

Correct Wrist Cocking

Many golfers have heard of the importance of "cocking" and "uncocking" the wrists during the swing, but it's surprising how many don't understand exactly how this action should work. In the correct motion, the wrists should cock or hinge in an upward and downward fashion only, as shown. You should never consciously attempt to hinge your wrists in a side-to-side fashion, either swinging back or down through the ball. Any such motion does little to add speed to the clubhead at impact and makes returning the clubface squarely to the ball much more difficult. So, cock your wrists on the backswing and uncock them on the downswing in an up-and-down fashion only.

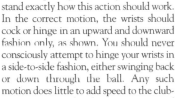

incorrect hinge

correct hinge

MASTER·STROKES

Create "Outside Feel" On Takeaway

The vast majority of amateurs pull the club back too abruptly inside the target line on the takeaway. This "fanning" movement starts a swing that's too flat, too much around the body.

Push the club away so that it feels as though you're moving the club "outside the target line." If you check your takeaway path in a mirror, you'll see that what feels like an outside takeaway, really starts the club straight back. This takeaway gets your arms extended for a wide, powerful arc.

"FEEL TAKEAWAY"

REAL TAKEAWAY

MASTER·STROKES

95°

70° ✓

Less Shoulder Turn Is OK

You always hear that a big shoulder turn is a "must" — 90 degrees from your address position or more. Many golfers lack the agility to do this, and in trying to make the big turn, will lose balance as they approach the top of the back-swing. Once this happens, the chances of returning the club precisely to impact are small.

Instead of straining for the big turn, accept your limitations. If the best turn you can make is 70 degrees from your starting position, you can still generate sufficient force to obtain good ball flight and distance. The key is to maintain good body control throughout all points in the swing, to give you the best possible chance for square contact.

MASTER STROKES

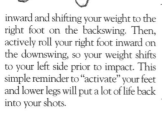

Active Feet = Lively Swing

If your golf swing and your shots have begun to look sluggish, a good place to look for the answer is your feet. Often, you'll fall into the habit of making a swing that utilizes the upper body only, while your feet and legs are "stuck in cement."

On the practice tee, hit some shots while focusing on rolling your left foot

inward and shifting your weight to the right foot on the backswing. Then, actively roll your right foot inward on the downswing, so your weight shifts to your left side prior to impact. This simple reminder to "activate" your feet and lower legs will put a lot of life back into your shots.

MASTER·STROKES

Make Club Feel "Light"

HANDS UNDERNEATH CLUB

CLUB PARALLEL TO TARGET LINE

At the top of the backswing, many amateurs swing the club into an off-balance position. The clubshaft is pointing at an angle to one side or the other of the target so that as you swing, the weight of the clubhead is out of control. If you get the sensation that the clubhead feels "heavy" at the top, it's probably out of position.

Practice getting the clubshaft to point directly parallel to your target line at the top of the backswing, with both hands directly underneath the club so that it feels well-supported, or "light." Then swinging the clubhead down freely and squarely into the ball will be much easier.

MASTER·STROKES

Match Swing Plane To Your Build

You often hear about the need for the swing to be "on plane." This refers to the steepness of the path that the clubhead revolves on around the body. Remember that there is no one correct plane for every golfer. However, the correct plane should match each individual's build.

If you are short and stocky, you'll need to stand a little farther from the ball. This means that your shoulders will turn on a plane more level to the ground, and therefore the club should also revolve on a relatively flat plane. If you are tall and slender, you'll stand closer to the ball at address. Your shoulders and the club should then move on a more upright plane.

More Upright

Flatter

MASTER·STROKES

"Replace" Your Hip

Most amateur golfers need to make as large a body turn as they can to generate power. Here's a useful swing image, particularly on tee shots: Imagine that on your backswing, you are going to take your left hip pocket and "replace" it to where your right hip pocket is positioned!

This simple image (even though your left hip really won't go that far) ensures that you will make the maximum possible hip turn on the backswing. And, when you make your maximum hip turn, it allows your shoulders to turn much farther than they could if your lower body remained static. Greater clubhead speed at impact will result.

RIGHT POCKET

LEFT POCKET

MASTER·STROKES

Let The Right Elbow "Float"

You may have heard the advice to keep your elbow "tight" to your right side on the backswing. To an extent this is good advice. However, golfers who focus on keeping the right elbow touching their right side will end up with a swing arc that is very narrow. This can hurt seniors in particular, because a too-narrow swing arc costs clubhead speed and distance they badly need.

On the practice tee, keep your right arm relaxed and allow your right elbow to "float" a couple of inches away from you on the backswing, rather than keeping it pinned. This slight adjustment will allow you to build a swing arc with a wider radius, which in turn gives your swing maximum power.

No

Yes

MASTER·STROKES

Concave Left Wrist Okay

You may have heard the advice that you should keep a "flat left wrist" throughout the swing. This flat position is easiest to see at the top of the backswing. However, it takes a fair amount of strength to maintain this flat left wrist, particularly at the top. For most golfers, it is also acceptable if the left wrist is in a slightly concave position, that is, a bit cupped in. A slightly concave position assures that both hands are underneath the club so it is well supported. On the other hand, avoid a convex left wrist at the top, meaning the wrist bows outward. From here, the weight of the club is hanging more "behind" the hands and it requires great strength and timing to get the club under control on the downswing. So if anything, err toward a concave left wrist.

CUPPED

FLAT

BOWED X

MASTER·STROKES

Right Arm Above Left

A common swing flaw is to whip the clubhead too quickly inside the target line at the start of the backswing. This "flat" backswing can cause numerous problems, accuracy being the biggest.

Here's a swing check you can observe by looking in a mirror, or have a friend observe on the practice tee: Take the club away until the clubshaft is parallel to the ground behind you. At this point, your right forearm should be slightly above your left. If the left forearm blocks any view of the right, it means you've pulled the clubhead to the inside too quickly.

MASTER·STROKES

Make A "T" At the Top

Many amateurs swing on a too-upright plane with the left shoulder dipping on the backswing, and the right shoulder dipping on the downswing. Such movements lead to "fat" shots with the clubhead digging too deep at impact, and also to shoulder and back problems.

Here's a tip to stay on-plane: As you swing to the top, keep both shoulders at right angles to your spine. Lines across your shoulders and spine should form a letter "T."

Practice obtaining this "T" at the top and you'll deliver the club on a shallower path for cleaner contact—and your back will stay healthier too.

The Full Swing

MASTER·STROKES

Butt of Club Points To Ball

You may have heard about the need to keep the club "on plane" throughout the swing. A swing that's too "flat," too much around the body, makes it difficult to hit the ball on-line. If your swing is too "upright" or too much up-and-down, you'll have trouble with hitting shots that are "fat" or "thin." A plane checkpoint: Have a friend observe your backswing at about the three-quarters position, when the clubshaft is pointing down. If the butt of the club is pointing beyond or outside the ball, you're in a too-flat position. If the butt points inside the ball, your plane is too upright. Practice swinging up to an on-plane position with the butt pointing right to the ball. Once you achieve it, your shotmaking will improve dramatically.

MASTER STROKES

Cock Wrists At the Top

The wrists are one of the "power levers" of the swing. As such, you want to cock the wrists fully as you approach the top of the backswing, particularly with the driver. Here are two tips to help you do this: **1.** Grip lightly at address and keep that light feel as you draw the club back. If the grip is tight, your wrists can't cock as freely. **2.** Imagine that at the top, you want to keep the clubshaft underneath an overhead object, say a chandelier. You'll need to cock the wrists fully to stay underneath it. **Final tip:** As you cock the wrists, strive to keep the back of the left hand flat or in line with your forearm. This helps keep the clubface square at impact.

MASTER·STROKES

More
body
turn,
less
arms

Don't Let Arms Outrun Body

Many golfers get in the habit of swinging too much with their arms, without enough turn of the body. This is often referred to as letting your arms "outrun" your body turn. Not only will such a swing lack power, but over time such a move can lead to injury of the rotator cuff in the left shoulder.

Execute your backswing by turning your body fully, rather than just trying to swing your arms as far as you can. The arms should feel passive — don't worry about how far back the club goes. You'll find you can obtain surprising power by turning a little more while keeping your arms and the club under control.

MASTER·STROKES

Turn Over Your Right Leg

In order to hit shots powerfully, it's important for golfers to use their body weight effectively. This means getting their weight "behind" the ball on the backswing, so that they can shift their weight aggressively onto the front foot and build clubhead speed through impact.

As you take the club back, try to turn your upper body so that at the top, the middle of your chest is directly over your right leg. You can tell if you are making this move correctly because you should feel pressure or tension in your right thigh. You are now in a position to shift your weight back to the left as you simultaneously drive the club through the impact zone with your upper right side.

MASTER·STROKES

Back To Target

In the most effective swings, the large muscles control the motion. A simple key to help utilize your body rather than your hands to execute the backswing is this: Turn your back to the target. You want to coil your upper body as fully as you can so that at the top, your shoulder blades point directly at the target. It's okay if you can't turn this far, as long as you turn as fully as you can while maintaining balance.

An added benefit of this swing tip is that it's almost impossible to make a fast backswing while thinking of turning your back to the target. You'll get the best windup you're capable of with a dependable swing tempo to boot.

Target

Back towards target

MASTER·STROKES

How Much Heel Lift?

Amateurs often ask, "How much should the left heel lift on the backswing?" The heel should lift as a reaction to the turning of the upper body and hips. Never make a conscious effort to lift the heel. Also, the more supple golfer will have less heel lift than the inflexible one. That said, many amateurs make a lazy, "flat-footed" swing in which the foot stays virtually flat to the ground. A minority, on the other hand, consciously lift the heel way off the ground so that only their left toe touches.

This is very undesirable as it causes you to sway to the right and lose balance. If you make a good, full body turn, your left ankle should turn inward with the heel rising one-half to one inch off the ground.

NO

NO

YES

The Full Swing

MASTER·STROKES

Keep Clubhead On Plane

Many amateurs worry about where to swing their arms, when and how to cock their wrists, and end up confused. A helpful backswing thought: Make the clubhead swing up on a straight circular plane such as defined by a hula hoop. When the swing is off-plane, it means the clubhead is moving either below or above the "hoop" (or sometimes both above and below at different points in the swing).

Practice your backswing slowly while watching in a mirror. Make the clubhead move back along a straight path, rather than looping inside, outside or both. Get accustomed to the movements needed to keep the clubhead moving on plane. Soon you'll take this on-plane backswing to the course, resulting in a swing that conserves energy and delivers clubhead to ball more consistently.

MASTER·STROKES

Tie Your Arms Together

Many higher-handicap golfers swing the club with their arms "disconnected." That is, the space between the arms increases because the right arm dominates the backswing and pulls away from the body.

To build a more effective swing that uses the entire body, keep the forearms close together and in front of the torso throughout the swing. Imagine that your forearms are tied together just below the elbows with a rope. In this condition, your arms are forced to remain close together throughout the backswing, as they should. This, in turn, will encourage you to use your torso to make a complete backswing turn. The end result is greater power and consistency.

MASTER·STROKES

When Is the Swing "Full"?

You may have heard that at the top of the swing, the clubshaft should be parallel to the ground. Many golfers who try to achieve this position shouldn't.

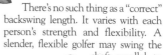

There's no such thing as a "correct" backswing length. It varies with each person's strength and flexibility. A slender, flexible golfer may swing the shaft parallel to the ground, or beyond. Meanwhile, for a thick-set player who can't turn the torso as far, a position in which the clubshaft is halfway between perpendicular and parallel to the ground is fine.

Studies have shown that a longer backswing does not always mean more distance. So, never try for a backswing that's longer than you're capable of.

MASTER·STROKES

Stop Wobbling At The Top

No

Many times you'll see a golfer whose hands and club seem to waver or wobble at the top of the backswing. Perhaps this is happening to you as well.

This wobbling at the top is a result of trying to swing back too far. In effect, the right hand and arm are trying to pull the left arm and the club farther back than they can comfortably reach. This extra "pull" to the top causes the club to wobble and also starts to pull your lower body off-balance. Result: erratic shots.

The solution is simple: Swing back only as far as your left arm and hand can comfortably go. Never try to reach back for more. You'll see that the clubshaft comes to a firm stop at the top, and you're poised and in balance for the downswing.

MASTER·STROKES

A Foolproof Check For Over-Swinging

Many golfers over-swing in a faulty attempt to develop power, and don't know they are doing so. Here's a great way to check. Set up at address with only your right hand on the club. Take the club all the way to the top with your right hand. Next, reach up with your left hand. Can you place your left hand exactly where it belongs on the handle? If you can't, it means that your right side has pulled you farther than your left side can reach. You'll be fighting yourself and pulling yourself off-balance at the top.

Practice swinging back with your right arm only as far as your left arm can comfortably reach back. You'll be in balance and hit the ball more consistently.

MASTER·STROKES

"Rest"

Set Clubhead On A Pillow

A very common error, particularly among amateurs, is to rush the swing, particularly in the transition from backswing to downswing. Rushing this transition causes loss of clubhead control, so that all kind of mis-hit shots can occur.

To help this problem, use this image: As you take the club back, imagine that you want to set the clubhead on a pillow for a brief "rest" at the top of the backswing. By keeping the simple visual image in mind, you will swing the club "quietly" and under control to the top. From there it will be much easier to start the club down smoothly and with increasing acceleration into the ball.

MASTER·STROKES

Start Downswing Slowly

It's true that really big hitters such as Tiger Woods generate a great deal of speed right from the top of the backswing. However for most amateurs, and particularly seniors, starting the downswing with a rush of effort will be disastrous as it can cause a lesser athlete to lose balance.

You will be far better off if you strive to start your downswing with slow, smooth, flowing movements with your arms, legs and hands. Staying slow and smooth and letting the momentum build toward impact will allow you to stay in much better balance through impact. This in turn greatly increases your chances of meeting the ball squarely and getting maximum distance and accuracy.

MASTER STROKES

The Inside Loop

Many amateurs constantly slice their shots because of a downswing path that delivers the club from the outside-in. A last-ditch solution: Make an "inside loop" on your downswing.

To create the inside loop, first swing the club up on a path that feels more to the outside than normal (as much as you can while retaining balance). Then, start down by consciously "looping" your hands, arms and the club well inside the path you took it back on. Keep turning your body through the shot and just "trust it." To the chronic slicer, the inside loop will feel odd at first. Practice it until you gain confidence before taking it on the course. Once there, the change in your ball flight will be dramatic!

MASTER·STROKES

Throw the Club Away!

The majority of amateurs over-control the club through the impact zone. They tense up and hold on too tightly, the result being that the clubface never gets squared up at impact. The result is weak, off-line shots to the right.

If you have this problem, here's what sounds like a radical cure: As you swing down, try to fling or throw the club away. That's right; swing as though you're going to let the club fly straight down the fairway! You won't actually do this, of course, but the key is to greatly decrease the tension in your hands and thus free up the clubhead. With this image in mind, you'll be amazed at how much more speed you generate and how much easier it is to square up the clubface.

MASTER STROKES

Time Your Downswing

Often, the timing of movements of the upper body (shoulders, chest and arms) does not blend with that of the lower body (hips and legs). Many amateurs move their hips and legs too fast on the downswing. This leaves the hands and arms behind so the clubface is open, resulting in a push or a slice. Some golfers throw their hands too quickly so the clubface moves too fast for the lower body. It closes by impact and a hook or smothered shot results.

If you're leaving the face open, make swings with your hands and arms starting the club down while your lower body feels "quiet." If your clubface is closed, start down by planting the left foot and sliding the left hip slightly toward the target. The correct adjustment will aid your timing and help deliver a square clubface at impact.

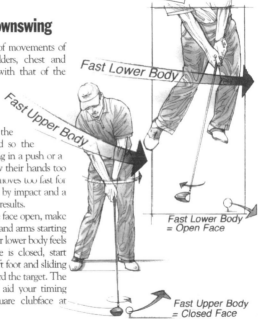

Fast Lower Body

Fast Upper Body

Fast Lower Body = Open Face

Fast Upper Body = Closed Face

MASTER·STROKES

Sweep, Don't Dig

The greatest energy is transferred from clubhead to ball when the clubhead is delivered while moving on a shallow rather than a steep downward path. You should work on keeping the arc of the swing as wide as possible. This gives you a shallower path at impact, as opposed to the steep downswing path you'll get by picking the club up abruptly on the backswing.

With a shallow swing path you'll get more solid-feeling impact, a more driving ball flight, and greater distance. Also, sweeping your shots puts much less stress on your joints and reduces the chance of injury.

SWEEP

MASTER·STROKES

Keep Knees Flexed Through Impact

Many golfers who top shots think it's because they've lifted their heads. Often the fault lies closer to the ground—their knees straighten at impact, so that the rest of the body is also raised, along with the club.

It takes some athletic ability and concentration to stay "flexed" throughout the swing, particularly for older golfers. **Two tips:** First, at address make sure your posture includes a slight rather than a deep knee flex. A slight flex is easier to maintain. Second, make a conscious effort to stay "sitting" or "level" through impact. Your thighs and rear will feel slightly heavy when you retain the knee flex. Train your knees to keep the same flex throughout and you'll find yourself hitting the ball solidly.

MASTER·STROKES

Extend Through The Impact Zone

Most amateurs try to steer the ball to the target rather than swinging their arms freely and trusting the swing to square the clubface. Steering leads to a loss of clubhead speed and power.

A great swing image is to get both arms fully extended just beyond impact. At a point in the swing with the clubhead two feet beyond impact, your arms should be fully extended so they form a letter "V" with the clubshaft pointing directly between the arms. On the practice tee, work on getting your arms into this fully extended position, and you'll whip the club through with a square clubface and maximum power.

MASTER·STROKES

Swing An Axe

Many golfers have been taught that for a right-hander, the left side must dominate the downswing. That is, the weight should shift rapidly to the left side, with the left arm pulling the club down.

For those of you looking for maximum power, consider this: If you wanted to deliver a level, powerful blow with an axe to a large tree, after swinging the axe back, would you merely shift your weight onto your left side and pull with your left arm? No! You would use the strength of your entire body, including your right arm, shoulder and side, to drive the axe into the tree trunk. Imagine this principle of swinging the axe next time you're on the course, and see if it doesn't add power to your shots.

Master Strokes

Follow Through Over A "Post"

Many golfers exhibit a follow-through in which the weight has shifted to the left leg, but the head and upper body are held in their original position so that the back is curved. This position, known as a "Reverse C," is especially hard on the back.

Instead of holding the upper body back, let your head and shoulders "flow" past the point of impact. In the follow-through, your head, shoulders and torso should be stacked directly over your left leg, forming a "post" with nearly all your weight supported by that leg. Such a move to the finish is healthier and will lead to more consistent shots as well.

MASTER·STROKES

"Fold Up" For On-Target Shots

A great many amateurs fail to "release" the club completely in the impact zone. They tend to "hold on" too long with the left arm extended, the result being that the clubface never gets back to square at impact and the ball flies to the right.

ELBOWS CLOSE TOGETHER

FOLD

Here's a tip to help square the clubface: Make practice swings in which both arms fold naturally at the elbows past impact, rather than the left arm remaining straight. Try to finish with your chest pointing at the target, and both elbows close together and folded so the clubhead falls directly behind you. You'll start seeing straighter shots as a result.

MASTER·STROKES

The 'Pocket-To-Pocket' Move

Older golfers in particular should strive to make as full a body turn as they can to help generate power, particularly on tee shots. Here's a useful swing thought to accomplish this: Imagine that as you swing back, you're going to take your left-side pants pocket and put it where your right pants pocket was before you started the swing. Even though your left hip won't turn as far as this image would suggest, this "pocket-to-pocket" move will ensure that you make your maximum possible hip turn on the backswing. Remember that maximizing your hip turn will automatically increase your shoulder turn as well. Greater clubhead speed at impact is your reward.

MASTER·STROKES

Hold Your Finish

Good balance is essential to consistent shotmaking. Here's a tip that will help you improve your balance, particularly when you're on the practice tee. With a driver or fairway metal-wood, hit your shot, and then hold your finish position for a count of three. This is not quite as easy as it sounds. In order to finish with good enough balance to hold your finish, you will have to develop a smooth, flowing downswing motion, with no lurching or excessive lateral movement (which usually are the result of trying to hit the shot too hard). Learn to hold your finish for a count of three and you'll see the improvement in your shotmaking consistency.

POWER KEYS

There is not a golfer in the world, from Tiger Woods on down, who would not like to hit the ball harder than they currently can. Never mind the fact that the ability to hit the ball farther, particularly with the driver, has less to do with good scoring than most people think! But to many recreational golfers, it's important to be able to look back on a round and, even if they've scored poorly, to be able to recall a couple of great drives, a par-4 reached with a drive and a wedge, or maybe even a par-5 reached in two shots. Following, then, are a baker's dozen plus a few extra lessons designed to help you develop your maximum possible clubhead speed—and power—at the moment of impact.

Section 4:

CONTENTS

MASTER·STROKES

Draw Shots For More Yardage

Players looking for extra distance off the tee should hit a draw which curves from right to left. It will always go farther than a shot that fades or slices to the right. A draw is hit with a slightly closed clubface, which in turn means that there is a little less loft at impact, resulting in a lower flight and some extra roll.

You can best achieve the draw from the tee by delivering the club-face to the ball with the club moving on a path from slightly inside the target line, and by releasing the clubhead freely through the ball. These two factors produce counter-clockwise sidespin and a right-to-left drawing flight.

MASTER·STROKES

Wider Stance For Longer Drives

For golfers searching for an extra 10 yards off the tee, here's a simple tip: Take a wider stance with your driver. Make sure to assume this wider stance by adjusting your right foot farther back at the address, about three to four inches. Meanwhile, keep your left foot in the same relative position so that the ball is on a line opposite your left heel to instep.

By adjusting your right foot back, you will automatically shift a higher percentage of your body weight behind the ball at address. This in turn will allow you to move more of your body weight through impact, adding clubhead speed and thus power.

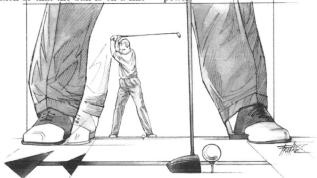

MASTER·STROKES

Shift Weight To Right

Many amateurs swing with their arms only. To maximize power, you must actively shift your body weight to your right side on the backswing, and then back to your left side on the downswing.

A good weight shift starts from the feet up. As you swing back, shift your weight onto your right foot. Don't stay flat-footed. Your left foot should roll onto its inside. And it's fine if your

weight shift pulls your left heel off the ground as you reach the top of the backswing. Remember that too much weight shift is better than none at all.

MASTER·STROKES

Soft Grip = Maximum Speed

Older golfers in particular need all the clubhead speed they can muster. A simple tip: For all regular full shots, grip the club as lightly as you can. You should just feel enough tension on the backswing to keep the club under control. As you move through impact, it should almost feel as if you're going to fling the club down the fairway. (Don't worry, you won't.)

By maintaining a light hold throughout the swing, you allow maximum freedom in your hands and arms, producing maximum speed through impact. A tight grip can only reduce the clubhead speed you generate.

Tight Grip

MASTER·STROKES

Turn Body Before Swinging Arms

The vast majority of amateurs swing the club too much with their hands and arms and too little via the turning of the body. This reduces both power and consistency. Here's a tip to help you: Start your swing by turning your midsection clockwise, or away from the target. Don't worry about making a specific move with your hands — they will move back with your torso. By getting your body turning immediately, you'll build much more tension during the backswing, which can then be unleashed on the way back down and through. Try this simple tip and see how much more power you can generate.

1st MOVE

MASTER·STROKES

Slow Down For Longer Drives

Most golfers confront a few holes each round where they need maximum distance off the tee to reach the green in regulation. The natural tendency to make a hard, fast swing, is the worst approach.

To maximize your power, make a conscious effort to draw the club back as slowly and as low to the ground as you can. This "low and slow" takeaway should feel exaggerated; you can't take the club back too slowly. By doing this, you create as wide a swing arc as possible, giving the club time to build momentum. And, you give yourself more time to make your maximum upper body turn away from the ball, so that you can "unfurl" on the down- swing and deliver maximum clubhead speed.

MASTER·STROKES

Use "Strong" Side
For Strong Start-Down

Right-handed golfers are often advised to start the downswing by pulling the club down with their left or "lead" arm. This is fine if your "strong" side is your left side. However, for the majority of people, the right side is their stronger side. It makes good sense to actively utilize your stronger right side to generate power in the downswing. So instead of "pulling" with the left, try this: Use your right leg to push your weight from your right foot onto your left, keeping your upper body passive for just an instant; then push your right shoulder, arm and the club-head through the impact zone. You may be surprised at the power you can generate.

MASTER·STROKES

Unlever The Right Arm

Many amateurs never utilize their right sides well and end up hitting weak shots, often pushed to the right.

Try this drill: On the practice tee, hold the club up in your right hand as shown, then throw or "unlever" your right arm without using any other part of your body. Can you feel the power generated as the clubhead moves quickly downward? Well, why not put that power into your swing? As you reach the top of your normal backswing, just think, "unlever the right arm" as you swing down. You'll build speed and power into your downswing, and will square the clubface better, too.

MASTER·STROKES

Drive Off An "Upslope"

Players who are not quite as strong as they once were, need to get as much carry as possible on their shots. Off the tee, you have the advantage of teeing the ball up, which allows you to sweep the ball into the air rather than hitting down on it.

When hitting a driver off the tee, imagine that you are standing on an upslope rather than flat ground, and that you want to swing the club "up the hill" through the impact zone. This image will help you to get your weight behind the ball at the top of the swing as it should be, then to sweep the club through the ball while utilizing the full loft of the clubface for maximum carry.

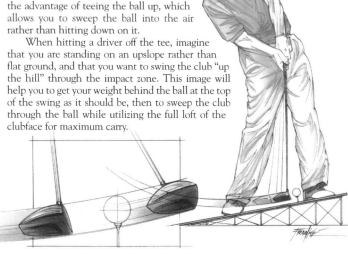

MASTER·STROKES

"Slam Door" on Downswing

The vast majority of amateurs push or slice their long shots. When this happens, they must be leaving the clubface pointing to the right at impact, or open in relation to the target.

If you're constantly pushing or slicing, imagine that on the downswing you are going to use your right hand and arm to "slam a door" at impact. It's as if the door's hinge is on your spine and the door jamb is in line with the ball. You must make the door slam at the instant your club reaches the ball. "Slam the door" aggressively, and you'll find that the ball will jump off your clubface with more force, and on target.

MASTER·STROKES

Right Over Left

A shot with a controlled, right-to-left draw will always provide a little more distance than a straight shot and a lot more than a slice. Here's a tip for developing your draw "action": On the practice tee using a middle iron, take half swings (hands moving from waist height to waist height). Grip the club lightly and focus on making your right forearm roll smoothly over your left in the impact zone, never rushing the action. You'll see that this easy "right over left" motion applies a touch of right-to-left draw spin to the ball. Gradually work this move into your full swing on the course, and you'll add distance to your shots.

MASTER STROKES

Pull With Arms, Turn With Hips

A good downswing blends forces that move vertically (up and down) and horizontally. Your arms pull the club down vertically while your hips and midsection turn horizontally. Start your downswing by pulling your arms and the club straight down behind you. Don't try to move them in the direction of the target. At the same time, turn your torso aggressively around toward the target, creating the horizontal force. The blending of downward pulling with the hands/arms and the turning of the body toward the target ensures a downswing that's on the correct inside-to-along-the-target-line path. It also provides maximum power at impact.

MASTER·STROKES

Drive Nail Into Back Of Ball

On tee shots in particular, you want to strike the ball with the clubhead moving as levelly as possible (as opposed to hitting down on it). This level blow imparts the greatest force and as a result, the longest carry.

On your tee shots, imagine that the point of a short nail is already in the back of the ball. As you swing down, try to drive that nail all the way through the ball. This image will automatically help you to coordinate your body's motion in such a way that you swing the clubhead more levelly through the impact zone. You'll enjoy the resulting flight and carry on your drives!

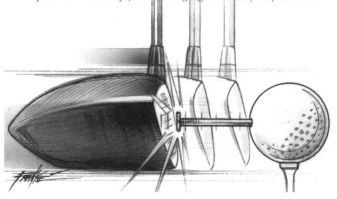

MASTER·STROKES

Make Forearms "Touch" Through Impact

Here's a simple tip that will help golfers who need to generate more clubhead speed through the impact zone: As you swing down, try to make your right or rear forearm catch up to and touch the inside of your left forearm. In actuality, you won't accomplish this. However, trying to make the right forearm catch up to the left will mean that you're speeding your entire right side through the ball as rapidly as possible. This will translate into maximum clubhead speed through the ball.

Practice some full shots using this image. You'll find yourself putting a lot more zip into your shots.

MASTER·STROKES

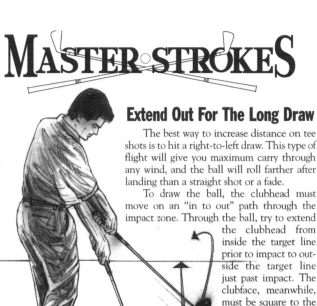

Extend Out For The Long Draw

The best way to increase distance on tee shots is to hit a right-to-left draw. This type of flight will give you maximum carry through any wind, and the ball will roll farther after landing than a straight shot or a fade.

To draw the ball, the clubhead must move on an "in to out" path through the impact zone. Through the ball, try to extend the clubhead from inside the target line prior to impact to outside the target line just past impact. The clubface, meanwhile, must be square to the target. The ball will start to the right of the target, and then draw back powerfully to the target line, and give you a nice long roll and extra distance.

MASTER·STROKES

Bang Your Back

So many golfers steer the clubhead through the ball, rather than swinging the club fully and freely. On driver tee shots, try this: As you execute the swing, focus on making the fullest possible follow-through. Try to make it so full that the club-shaft hits you in the back!

You may not build up enough speed and momentum in the clubhead and shaft for this to actually happen. However, by focusing on "banging your back" in the follow-through, you'll develop maximum speed through the impact zone.

Longer drives will definitely be the result.

MASTER STROKES

Swing "Through" the Ball

Many golfers become "ball bound," that is, they think in terms of swinging the club at the ball, not through it. This creates a quick, jerky action in which the clubhead is actually slowing down as it makes contact.

On all full shots, don't fixate on hitting the ball. Instead, think of making as full, free, and flowing a swing as you can. Imagine that the ball is simply an object in the way of your swing path, and you will swing right through it. With this approach you will generate maximum clubhead speed through impact, as well as hit your shots more squarely.

WHOOSH

MASTER·STROKES

Push Off The Block

To create maximum power, you need to use your entire body effectively, including the feet and lower legs. Here's a good drill to help you to utilize your leg power: Set a fairly small, heavy object like a concrete block in your back yard. Take your address position, and set your right foot at an angle against the block. As you make your backswing, you'll feel tension build up in your lower right leg. Then, start your downswing by pushing off with your right foot against the block. Repeat this drill about 25 times or until your right leg feels fatigued. Then, start working this movement into your swing on the course. You'll hit more powerful shots.

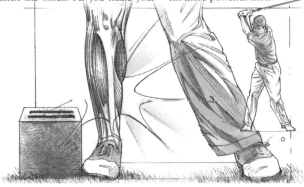

SHOTMAKING

The ability to be a shotmaker—to hit various types of altered or "special" full shots as opposed to taking a "pure vanilla" swing—is what separates the average golfer from the real "player." This section will show you the various adjustments needed to become a shotmaker. You can learn to draw or fade the ball to get it close to a tightly-guarded pin, how to hit the ball lower in strong winds, how to play shots from uneven lies, how to "take something off" a shot when necessary, and numerous other subtle tricks.

A word of warning, though: It's important that you develop and ingrain a consistent "basic" swing before you try to become a full-fledged shotmaker. If you are a beginner or high handicapper and are getting erratic results in your long game, you need to keep concentrating on the basics of the swing. Try to become a shotmaker very slowly and gradually

Section 5:

CONTENTS

MASTER·STROKES

Play Chip Shots With Your Irons

Too many golfers, when faced with an iron shot approach, make the mistake of swinging all-out. You should never do this because your goal is to hit the ball accurately, not far.

Try this experiment on the practice tee: Take out a 5-, 6- or 7-iron and aim at a target you can reach comfortably. Try to make what feels like a "chip shot" length swing. You'll probably be surprised to find that your "chip shot" swing is not only sending the ball on line to the target, but is also flying the ball all the way there! It's odd but true that when a golfer makes what feels like a tiny swing, he or she really makes a nice, controlled three-quarter swing at the ball. So, for pin-high control on your approach shots, think "chip shot" swing.

MASTER·STROKES

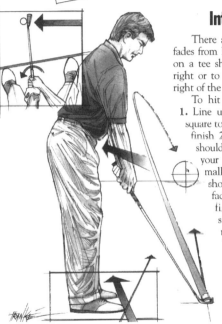

Intentional Fade

There are times when a shot that fades from left to right is useful, either on a tee shot to a fairway that bends right or to a well-guarded flag on the right of the green.

To hit a fade, do the following: 1. Line up leading edge of clubface square to where you want the shot to finish 2. Align feet, hips, knees and shoulders slightly open or left of your target line. 3. Swing normally along your body line. This should put a slight clockwise or fade spin on the ball. 4. If you find that your shots fly straight instead of fading, make one extra adjustment: Turn both your hands a shade to the left on the grip. This encourages a slightly more open clubface at impact, and more fade

FRANKE

MASTER STROKES

Analyze Your Ball Flight

There's no better way to spot swing flaws than to watch the ball fly. If the ball starts out straight at the target, your clubhead is moving correctly along the target line at impact. If the ball starts out to the right, your swing path is too much from the inside-out. If the ball starts left, your swing path is from the outside-in.

If the ball curves later in the flight, this shows how the clubface pointed at impact, in relation to the swing path. A ball that curves to the left (regardless of the starting path) shows that your clubface was closed. Any curve to the right indicates an open clubface. If the flight is continually straight, the clubface was square to the path of the swing at impact.

MASTER·STROKES

Soft Shot, Slow Tempo

You must pitch the ball over a greenside bunker and land it softly to stop it near the hole. How can you hit the high, soft lob like you see the pros do? Much of the secret lies in the swing tempo. Select your most-lofted club, setting up with the ball placed forward in your stance, so your hands are level with or slightly behind it. Make a long, very slow backswing. Then try to swing the club down just as slowly as you brought it back. You should feel as though your swing is longer than necessary, almost as though it's taking place "under water."

This ultra-slow tempo allows you to bring the clubhead through the ball on a very shallow arc, which in turn puts maximum loft on the clubface at impact.

SLOW

BALL FORWARD

OPEN STANCE

MASTER·STROKES

Choke Down For Greater Control

Here's a simple tip that many amateurs overlook: When playing a shot where accuracy rather than distance is the main concern, choke down on the grip slightly. This adjustment comes in most handy on short to middle iron shots (pitching wedge through 5-iron) where you have an opening to the flag, so that you don't have to hit the ball extra-high, and especially if the wind is blowing. Take one club longer than normal (say, a 7-iron instead of an 8-). Grip down the handle one inch. Then make your normal swing, within yourself and in good balance. Your chances of making solid contact are much higher; the resulting shot will fly a little lower than normal but holds its line to the flag.

MASTER·STROKES

Punch Shot Into Wind

When playing in windy conditions, it's important, especially for seniors, not to try to overpower the shot. A controlled swing and good balance are more essential than ever.

On approach into strong winds, play the punch shot. If you're a 7-iron distance from the green under calm conditions, take out a four-iron. Grip down on the shaft two inches. Position the ball in the middle of your stance, slightly farther back than normal. Make a three-quarter backswing, then hit down crisply and follow through with your club pointing toward the target. It should feel as though you're hitting an extra-long chip shot. The ball will take off low and straight and bore through the wind rather than being caught up in it.

choke down

MASTER·STROKES

Don't Overpower The Wedge

Many amateurs, mostly men, let their egos get in the way on short-iron approach shots. Influenced by how far the pros hit the ball, they'll try to hit a pitching wedge from 135 yards or a sand wedge from 115. Even if they could reach the green with these clubs from these distances, shots that require an all-out swing rarely if ever get the ball close.

Make it a rule that you will never swing at more than 85 percent effort with your 8-iron, 9-iron, pitching wedge or sand wedge. And, choose the club that will allow you to do that for the given shot. You'll find yourself hitting short approach irons consistently closer to the flag.

MASTER·STROKES

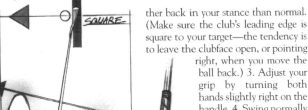

ther back in your stance than normal. (Make sure the club's leading edge is square to your target—the tendency is to leave the clubface open, or pointing right, when you move the ball back.) 3. Adjust your grip by turning both hands slightly right on the handle. 4. Swing normally and freely, releasing the club fully through impact. A low, strong, right-to-left shot will result.

The Low, Hard Draw

When it's windy and/or when the ground is firm, the low, right-to-left draw is very helpful. It stays lower because you strike the ball with a slightly closed clubface, and the counter-clockwise spin "fights" the wind. Also, the ball runs farther upon landing. To play the low draw, 1. Aim your body right of the target line. 2. Move the ball two to three inches far-

Shotmaking

MASTER·STROKES

The Big Slice

The big, lazy slice is the last thing most golfers want. However, it's useful to bend the ball around trees or other obstacles. Here's how to hit the intentional slice: Aim your clubface directly at your target (even if this means it's aiming at a tree that's in your way!) Align feet, knees, hips and shoulders well left of target. Make sure to swing along your body line, so the clubhead cuts sharply across the target line from outside to in. Hold on firmly with your left hand to assure that the clubface stays open in relation to your swing path. Result: a shot that starts well left, then bends toward the target. Note: Don't try the big slice unless you have a clean lie — grass between clubface and ball will keep the ball from curving.

MASTER·STROKES

"Tight Circle" On Short Irons

On approach shots of 150 yards or less, accuracy is paramount. You want to develop a controlled, in-balance swing in which you transfer less weight going back and coming down than you would with a full drive.

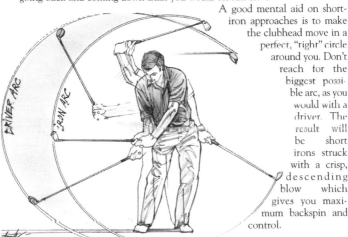

A good mental aid on short-iron approaches is to make the clubhead move in a perfect, "tight" circle around you. Don't reach for the biggest possible arc, as you would with a driver. The result will be short irons struck with a crisp, descending blow which gives you maximum backspin and control.

MASTER·STROKES

Curve Approaches "Into" Wind

It's tough to hit approach shots close when you're playing in crosswinds. If you can draw and fade the ball, here's where you should use that ability to save strokes.

Say the pin is located on the left side of the green and the wind is blowing left to right. A straight shot would be blown away from the flag and would roll farther right upon landing. Here, set up for a shot that starts just right of the hole, but with "draw" spin on it. This shot will hold its line in the crosswind, and will land softly because its curve will be "fighting" the wind. Final tip: Whether you're drawing or fading against the crosswind, take one club longer than normal to counteract the wind's effect on the shot.

MASTER·STROKES

Longer Club From Uphill Lie

Most amateurs underestimate the distance adjustment necessary for approach shots off uphill lies. Usually they take one club longer than normal, figuring this gives sufficient power to reach the elevated green.

However, most golfers forget that if the lie is uphill, this adds loft at impact, shortening the shot more than they'd think. Say you're playing from an upslope of 12 degrees. This means the ball will take off at an angle three clubs shorter than off a level lie (since the difference in loft between each club is about four degrees). So, if you are playing off an up-slope this steep, use an iron three clubs longer than normal (a 4-iron instead of a 7-iron), then swing normally.

24°

= 36

+12°

MASTER·STROKES

Bend Higher Leg on Uneven Lies

On many courses you'll encounter uphill or downhill lies on approach shots. These are tricky because it's easy to lose balance. On uphill lies you can fall back from the ball; on downhill lies, toward the target. The result can be badly mis-hit shots.

Whenever the lie is steep, at address, bend your "uphill" leg considerably more than your downhill leg. By doing this, your upper body weight will rest on a line that's more vertical, as opposed to leaning too much down the slope. This will greatly improve your balance during the swing. One final tip: From steep lies, take plenty of club so you can make an extra-smooth swing.

BEND
UPHILL
KNEE

MASTER·STROKES

Shot Curves From Sidehill Lies

When playing a hilly course, remember that sidehill fairway lies will cause the ball to curve. Assuming you normally hit the ball straight, when the ball is below your feet, the shot will fade or slice right. Bend your knees slightly more than usual to get the club down to the ball; and aim for the left edge of the green, allowing the shot to fade back toward the middle.

When the ball is above your feet, it will tend to hook left. Choke down on the club a bit to help you make better contact; aim for the right edge of the green as the ball will draw back toward green center. Final tip: The ball will run farther upon landing from this lie.

MASTER·STROKES

"Ride" The Wind

If you're playing on a gusty day, remember this: When the wind is blowing, the ball will fly much farther if it is spinning "with" the wind rather than "into" the wind. This is especially helpful to know on tee shots with a crossing wind. If the wind is blowing from left to right, align your body toward the left rough with the clubface aligned toward the fairway, then swing normally. This setup produces a shot that starts left but has left-to-right "fade" spin on it, so that it will "ride" that left-to-right wind. Reverse the procedure if the wind is right-to-left, so that you "draw" the shot the same way the wind is blowing. Understanding how to "ride the wind" off the tee can easily add 20 yards.

FRANKE

MASTER·STROKES

Use Tee On Par-3s

On par-3 holes, you'll sometimes see a player drop the ball onto the grass of the teeing area and hit the shot as from the fairway. However, you should always tee up the ball on par-3 holes. If hitting a longer iron (2- through 5-iron), tee the ball one-quarter to one-half inch above the ground. For a shorter shot (6-iron through wedge), tee the ball no more than one-quarter inch. Teeing the ball up slightly always gives you a better opportunity to get "all" of the ball for maximum carry and height. Also, by teeing the ball you eliminate the possibility of grass getting between club and ball at impact, which can cause the shot to "fly" and have less backspin upon landing.

Shotmaking

MASTER·STROKES

When Not Teeing Can Help You

Sometimes you will face a tight tee shot where you'd like to hit a 3- or 5-wood for accuracy. However, the wind is against you, so that it will be hard to get much distance with these clubs. Also, the wind can blow more lofted shots off-line.

Here's a great tip for these situations. Take your fairway metal-wood as planned. Instead of teeing the ball up, place it on the grass so that it's sitting well, but with a little bit of grass behind the ball. Tee off from this lie. Because some grass will get between clubface and ball at impact, you won't get much backspin on the shot. The shot will fly lower and cut through the wind, it won't hook or slice as much, and it will give you more roll than normal upon landing.

WIND

MASTER STROKES

Play "Straight" When It's Wet

In wet weather conditions, the clubface will not be able to "grip" the ball as it would when it's dry. This means the ball will have less backspin and also less sidespin than normal. Generally, lack of backspin is not a problem because the ball will stop quickly once it hits the wet, soft ground. However, keep in mind that in the wet it's very hard to play "special" approach shots that either draw or fade toward your target. So when it's wet, play simple shots. Aim for the spot on the fairway or green you want to hit, rather than trying to draw or fade the ball in, because a wet clubface and ball will always produce a much straighter-flying shot.

MASTER·STROKES

Driver From Fairway

Under the right conditions, a driver from the fairway can be a stroke-saver—you may reach the green on a par 5 or a long par 4 that you couldn't otherwise. But it is a tactic that only players who generate high clubhead speed should use. If you can't carry the ball over 200 yards off a tee with a driver while obtaining a good high trajectory, don't try it from the fairway.

Other points for judging whether to hit the driver off the fairway: The lie must be very clean with some cushion underneath the ball; the lie should be flat or uphill, never downhill; and the wind, if any, should be against you, which helps in getting the shot airborne.

"DRIVER"   GOOD LIE ONLY

MASTER·STROKES

When To Hit An Iron Hard

Sometimes you'll find yourself "between clubs," needing, say, a smooth 6-iron or a hard 7-. Most times, you're better off taking the longer club and easier swing. However, there are times to use a shorter club and harder swing. Usually this is when the pin is on the front, guarded by a trap that's not too difficult to escape from. The smooth 6-iron should reach the green easily; however, with the softer swing, the ball carries less backspin so it "releases" to the back of the green. If you go with the hard 7-, the ball should fly to the front, but the harder swing with increased loft means the ball will land more steeply and with much more backspin—stopping it near the hole.

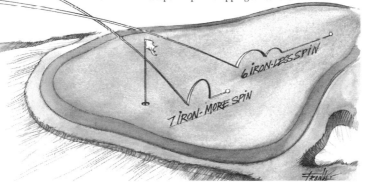

MASTER·STROKES

PLAN →

"B"

ALIGN LEFT

EXTEND TOWARD TARGET

A Useful "Plan B" Shot

Everyone has days when their full swing isn't at its best. It's good to have a "Plan B" type shot for these off-days. Here's how to play a Plan B or "block" shot, either from tee or fairway: Set clubface square to target, but align your entire body slightly to the left. Make a relatively short, controlled backswing. On the downswing, pull the clubhead down the target line, holding on firmly with the left hand. Keep the clubhead moving low and along the target line for longer than normal past impact. Thus you won't be releasing as freely through impact as with your normal swing. Your shots will fly a little lower, either straight or with a slight fade to the right. It's a great way to keep the ball on-target.

MASTER·STROKES

3/4 back

choke
up 2"

low tee

2"back

Low Driver Into the Wind

One of the tougher shots in golf is the tee shot directly into a strong wind. The overwhelming tendency is to try to overpower the shot, but here's how to adjust: First, tee the ball just a little lower than normal. Next, position the ball one ball-width back in your stance (just inside a line to your left heel). Third, grip down one to two inches. Fourth, make a compact swing with little body movement that feels like only a 3/4 effort. You'll be surprised to find that the ball starts like a low bullet, stays low, and has less backspin than your normal drive. It will run farther upon landing so that you end up with maximum distance into the wind—as well as much better control.

MASTER·STROKES

The Wedge Punch

A great shot to have from about 75 to 100 yards out, especially when it's windy, is the low, "punched" wedge shot. First, position the ball behind the center of your stance with your hands ahead. The clubface should be square to the target and slightly de-lofted. Next, make a three-quarter swing mainly with your arms and with little body movement.

Hit down sharply into the back of the ball and follow through low, with your hands and the clubhead pointing to the target. The ball will fly lower than a normal wedge shot, so you have great control. But it will also carry more backspin than a high wedge shot, so you can still stop it faster than you'd think.

MASTER·STROKES

Hit Approach Clubs 10 Yards Shorter

A lot of amateurs are overly concerned with hitting irons long distances. They think they should hit a 5-iron over 200 yards like the pros sometimes can. But "swinging for the fences" is the worst thing you can do. You'll find that on average you'll get the ball closer when you swing with less than full effort.

Let's say that if you make a full swing and get perfect contact, you can hit a 5-iron 170 yards. On the course, make it a rule that you will use your 5-iron from 160 yards, making a very smooth, controlled motion. Use this same swing force with your irons from all distances, hitting 10 yards less than your maximum, and you'll hit many more greens.

200yds

160 yds

MASTER STROKES

'Clip' Your Iron Shots

You've often been told to "hit down" on your iron shots, digging a substantial divot beyond impact. However, keep in mind that hitting down sharply puts great strain on the hands and wrists and can easily lead to injury. Second, a steep descent increases the chances of hitting the shot "fat."

On the practice tee, work on creating a circular path of the clubhead through the hitting zone, rather than a steep V-shaped path. Position the ball between the center of your stance and a line opposite your left heel. You'll contact the ball with the clubhead just moving slightly downward to its lowest point, which is just past the ball. Clean, solid shots will result.

NO

YES

SHALLOW DIVOT

MASTER·STROKES

Adjustments For High, Soft Approach

SHALLOW

Ball forward

path

target

There are times, such as when the wind is behind you, when you'll need a high, soft iron shot to hold the ball on the green. Here are adjustments that will help: First, select one club longer than you ordinarily would. Align the clubface square to target, then set your body line slightly left of target. This positions you to make a swing that cuts across the ball slightly from outside to inside, putting a fade spin on the ball that makes it fly higher and land softer. Also, position the ball one ball-width more forward than normal in your stance. This allows contact at the bottom of the swing arc rather than while hitting down, adding loft at impact. Finally, maintain an extra slow, smooth rhythm. You'll like the flight you see.

Shotmaking

MASTER·STROKES

Thin To Win

You've probably heard of "thin" or "fat" iron shots. A thin shot is one where the clubface makes contact a little higher on the ball than desired. Fat contact means the leading edge contacts the ground before the ball.

You're much better off hitting a shot slightly thin than fat. Assuming you make contact as shown, the ball will fly a little lower than if you had struck it perfectly, will travel just about normal distance, and will still have some backspin. The fat shot, on the other hand, will almost always come up short. Also, because the club contacts the ground first, it's more likely the clubface will be jarred off-line. All this is why pros use the phrase, "Thin to Win." A tip to avoid hitting fat shots: Concentrate on the top of the ball, rather than the back of it, as you swing.

THIN

toWin

MASTER·STROKES

Tilt Tee For Draw Or Fade

You're on the tee of a dogleg par-four. If you can hit a controlled draw (on dogleg left) or fade (on dogleg right) you'll cut yardage off the hole and stay in the fairway more easily. Here's a little-known tip to help you curve the ball: When you tee up, tilt the tee slightly in the direction you want the ball to curve. If you want the ball to draw left, tilt the tee to the left; for a fade right, tilt the tee right. As the ball takes off, it will pick up a little more sidespin to move it in the direction you want. Finally, to draw the shot, tee a bit higher than normal as well as tilting the tee left. To fade the shot, tee a shade lower as well as tilting the tee right.

Draw

Fade

MASTER·STROKES

Shots "Fly" From Light Rough

Every golfer should know the distances he or she averages with the various clubs. But do you know that, depending on the lie, shots may travel much farther than average?

Say, for example, you expect to hit a 6-iron 150 yards from a perfect fairway lie. But your ball is lying in light rough, so some grass will get between clubface and ball at impact. This means the shot will "fly": It will take off with less backspin, carry a little farther than normal, and then roll more upon landing. You will probably get 165 to 170 yards from the shot in this case, so plan for it when selecting your club.

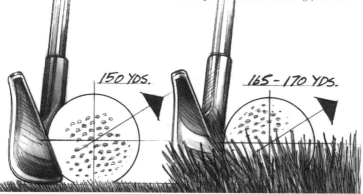

MASTER·STROKES

Improvise With Fewer Clubs

The golfer who can hit more than one basic shot has an advantage, since any given shot may require something a little different to make the ball finish at the target. So, a good way to increase your shotmaking capability is as follows: When you go out for a casual nine holes, carry half your set (say a 3-wood, 7-wood, 5-, 7-, 9-irons, sand wedge and putter). You'll need to improvise to get a little more or less distance out of a given club, hit it higher or lower, or make it stop a little faster or roll more. This exercise will teach you a lot about making fine adjustments to your swing. You may even find out you can score better while using fewer clubs!

MASTER·STROKES

Handling In-Between Wedge Distances

Many amateurs have problems controlling distance on fairway shots with the pitching wedge or sand wedge. Often this is because there is a large difference between the lofts on these clubs. Thus you may hit a full pitching wedge 115 yards but your sand wedge only, say, 90. When you have an approach in that 100-105 yard range, or a shot of 70-80 yards with the sand wedge, do this: Rather than trying to judge the lesser amount of swing you'll need, grip down one to two inches, then make a normal, smooth swing. Gripping down one inch will take 5-6 yards off the shot, and by two inches, about 10-12 yards. This simple adjustment will allow you to reduce your yardage on these in-between distances, without adjusting your swing.

2" = 10-12 YDS. OFF

1" = 5-6 YDS. OFF

FULL WEDGE

MASTER·STROKES

Less Club, Firm Swing With Wind

You've probably heard the advice to take plenty of extra club when you're hitting approach shots into the wind. What about when you have an iron shot to a well-guarded green, and a strong breeze is at your back? In this case, your best bet is to take a shorter club (one, two, or three clubs less than normal, depending on the wind's strength), and make a full swing at the ball. By taking a shorter club and swinging firmly, you'll get the most height and maximum backspin on the ball, giving you the best chance to carry the ball to the front of the green and stop it on the surface.

MASTER·STROKES

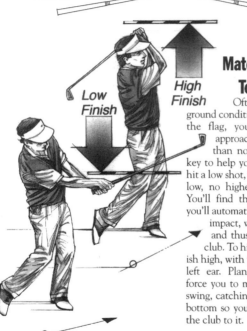

Low
Finish

High
Finish

Match Swing Finish
To Desired Flight

Often, because of wind or ground conditions, or the location of the flag, you'll need to hit an approach shot higher or lower than normal. Here's a simple key to help you accomplish this: To hit a low shot, finish with your hands low, no higher than chest height. You'll find that by using this key you'll automatically "trap" the ball at impact, with the hands leading and thus with less loft on the club. To hit a high approach, finish high, with your hands above your left ear. Planning this finish will force you to make a more sweeping swing, catching the ball right at the bottom so you apply the full loft of the club to it.

TROUBLE PLAY

The trouble play section is an extension of the previous section on shotmaking. The advice described deals with more extreme situations—shots where you need to escape from real trouble. These situations include unusual lies of the ball, odd stances with the ball well above or below your feet, shots where your backswing is limited by a tree, even shots that you have to play left-handed (assuming you're a righty)!

Oftentimes when the handicap amateur runs into a difficult trouble shot, he or she tries to hit a miracle shot all the way to the green. The results are almost always disastrous, leading to the really big score on one hole that can ruin a good round. Learning the correct techniques for these difficult shots, as well as taking a more prudent approach as to the results you should expect, can help you avoid these disasters.

Section 6:
CONTENTS

MASTER·STROKES

Use Extra Loft From Rough

If you've lost a little clubhead speed, the place where it will show up the most is when you're trying to escape from rough. When the ball is nestled down, the grass will wrap around the club's hosel at impact, slowing it and "closing" the clubface so that there's not nearly enough loft on the club to get the ball out.

When stuck in sticky rough, assess the lie, then choose an iron that has a loft two clubs higher than you need. For example, if you think you can get it out with a 5-iron, use a 7-iron instead. Since the ball will come out lower and with more roll than usual, you'll be pleasantly surprised with the results.

MASTER·STROKES

Adjust From Fairway Bunkers

Most amateurs have trouble making good contact from fairway bunkers. Here are a couple of setup tips that will help.

First, since you must dig your feet into the sand for a secure stance, you're a little lower than normal in relation to the ball. So

GRIP DOWN

AIM RIGHT

MOVE BALL BACK

you'll automatically tend to hit the shot "fat." Adjust by gripping down the handle three-quarters of an inch. Also, because your feet are lower than the ball, your swing will be flatter than normal, which can cause a pull or hook. So, close your stance so that your aim is a little right of the target. Finally, position the ball about one ball-width back in your stance from its normal position to help assure that you catch the ball first.

MASTER·STROKES

Precision Punch
From Pine Needles

In many areas, when you hit an errant tee shot you'll find yourself in a pine forest, your escape to be played off pine needles. The shot is not difficult with a few adjustments. Address the ball with 75 percent of your weight on your left foot. Move the ball back about four inches in your stance, to just behind center. This de-lofts the clubface, so use one club shorter than normal (a 6-iron instead of a 5-).

Limit your backswing to three-quarter length, with little weight shift. This will keep you in balance even on slick pine needles, and help you catch the ball first with a descending blow. Finish low with clubshaft pointing to target. The ball will start out low, helping you keep it under any branches, but it will have much more backspin than you'd get from normal rough.

3/4

75%

MASTER·STROKES

3/4 swing

choke down

Under The Branches

Sometimes you'll find your approach shot blocked by tree branches. You must go under them because you're too close to get the ball over. When hitting under branches, remember the following:

1. Assess the starting flight needed to keep the ball under the branches. Select a low-enough-lofted iron to accomplish this.

2. Grip down two inches; position the ball back of center in your stance; hit down firmly with a controlled three-quarter swing.

3. Beware if your ball is lying in deep rough. You must use enough loft to get the ball out of it, so it may be impossible to keep it under the branches. The best move here is to pitch back safely to the fairway.

MASTER STROKES

The Left-Handed Recovery

There will be a time when you need to play out of trouble such as near a tree trunk, by swinging left-handed (for a right-handed player). Some tips to help you escape: **1)** Select a long iron (2-, 3- or 4-) which you will play with the face turned upside-down. These clubs have less loft, so the ball won't shoot out too much to the right when the face is upside down. **2)** Reverse the position of your hands on the club; grip well down the handle for more control. **3)** Take two or three "chip shot" length practice swings to get a feel for the motion. **4)** Aim to hit a short distance back into the fairway — never try a "full" shot. **5)** Keep head and body still throughout the stroke. **6)** Practice the lefty recovery shot a few times, before you actually need it!

reverse hands

MASTER·STROKES

Extra Loft From Downhill Lie

Approach shots from downhill lies are difficult for all players, especially seniors who often have trouble lofting their shots. From a severe (12°) downhill lie, remember that you must take a shorter club, with more loft than the distance would call for from a level lie. If you are a 5-iron distance from the green and you are playing from a steep downslope, use no more than a 7-iron. Swing down and through the shot rather than trying to lift it. Because of the downslope you're on, the 7-iron face will move through impact with the loft of no more than a 5-iron. Always remember that when in doubt from downhill lies, take the more-lofted club.

$$37° - 12° = 25°$$

MASTER·STROKES

Stance In Trap, Ball Out

Your tee shot reaches the edge of a fairway bunker. Your stance is in the sand, the ball in thick rough well above your feet. This is a difficult shot, but here's how to make the most of it:

1. Assess the lie. Let's say that if the lie were level, the least loft you could escape with is a 7-iron. In this case, take one more lofted club (8-iron) since from this severe sidehill lie the clubface will close at impact, reducing loft.

2. Choke down on grip; stand "tall" to the ball.

3. Aim to right of intended target: There's a strong tendency to pull or hook.

4. Make three-quarter arm swing while keeping body still. Never try to "force" this shot all the way to the green with a longer club and bigger swing.

choke down

use more loft

little knee flex

MASTER·STROKES

STEEP

Hitting From a Divot Hole

After a good drive, you find your ball lying in a divot hole. While this complicates matters, it doesn't mean you have to lose a stroke. Here are adjustments to help you hit the green: First, take one club longer than normal, say a 6-iron instead of a 7-iron. Choke down on the grip at least one inch this automatically gives you a narrower swing arc and more control. Position the ball a little farther back, toward stance center, and keep a little more weight than normal on your left side. Make an upright backswing, then swing down sharply into the back of the ball. This steep contact will give you an abbreviated, "punch" type finish. The ball will come out lower than normal, so if there's room try to land the ball just short of the green.

choke down

Ball back

MASTER STROKES

Ball Pinned Against Back Lip

Your ball has stopped against the back lip of a greenside bunker — an extremely tough shot. You would need to swing straight up and down to get your clubhead to enter the sand behind the ball. Even then, you risk catching the back lip on the way down, so you leave the ball in the bunker or even whiff the shot. What can you do?

In severe cases like this, take an alternate escape route. Forget shooting for the flag. Aim away so you can avoid the back lip and swing into the sand at a more normal angle. Most often you should aim toward the front of the green, or maybe the fairway in front of it. Then play a normal sand shot to there. If you can get down in a total of three, you've done as well as you can hope from this tough spot.

MASTER·STROKES

Upright Swing From Deep Rough

Steeper

Escaping deep rough is especially tough on golfers who may not generate great clubhead speed. Here's a tip that will help you out of rough: Make a more upright swing than normal. First, stand an inch or two closer to the ball at address. Then push the club straight back and stretch your arms high on the backswing (as opposed to swinging your arms around your body). Swing down along the same steeper-than-normal path. The club will descend more directly down on the ball, meeting less resistance from the grass than it would if you swung on a shallower plane. You'll carry the ball higher and further from deep rough.

closer to ball

MASTER·STROKES

When You're "Up A Tree"

Every now and then you find your ball close to a tree trunk, severely limiting your backswing or downswing. The tendency is to try to get too much from these recoveries. The result can be a muffed shot, or even a whiff. Take a few practice swings to get the feel of how far back or through you can take the club. Once you've gained this feel, hit the shot with a normal amount of force for the amount of swing available. Don't try to put something "extra" into the downswing. This may mean you can only advance the ball 30 or 40 yards. If so, that's fine. Lastly, aim your recovery so that you definitely get it back to the fairway.

MASTER·STROKES

Use Ample Loft
From Fairway Bunkers

Long shots from fairway bunkers are difficult for most players. Since the ball is lying "tight" on the sand, there's no cushion, and thus little room for error in contact. It's tough to get the ball well up in the air from these lies, especially for seniors who generate lower clubhead speeds.

When sizing up fairway bunker shots, take a club with enough loft. Unless your lie is extremely good, select no longer than a 5-iron, even if that means you can't get the ball all the way to the green. The shorter clubshaft and loft of the 5-iron (or higher) give you a better chance to swing in balance and get the ball well up and out, with at least a fighting chance to save par

NOT ENOUGH LOFT

MORE LOFT

MASTER·STROKES

Don't Try It Till You've Practiced It

Occasionally, you'll find yourself facing a very unusual shot. For example, you may have to play the shot left-handed; or stand inside a deep bunker with the ball outside it, way above your feet; or you may be standing well above the ball, which is in the edge of a water hazard.

When you encounter a situation requiring a very odd swing, the best advice is not to try a full shot unless you have practiced the situation. If you haven't "felt" the swing that's needed, you might hit into more trouble or even whiff the shot. Instead, play a safe chip into the fairway and go from there, or take an unplayable lie penalty if necessary. Later, practice these situations when playing a few casual holes, so you're more prepared for them in the future.

THE SHORT GAME: WEDGING AND CHIPPING

This important section deals with the shots played from off the green with less than a full swing—from, say, 75 yards in to the flag. This is the most artistic area of the game of golf, where your creativity, awareness of course contours, and your touch are tested in an infinite variety of ways. Your goal in the short game is to learn to turn three shots into two by hitting a chip or pitch shot close enough to the hole to leave you with a very short, makeable putt.

Study the lessons in this section carefully. Because power is not much of a factor in the short game, success on these shots is within every player's reach. And, mastery of the short game is the quickest route to lower scores.

Section 7:

CONTENTS

MASTER·STROKES

Check Your Chipping Technique

On short greenside chips, you want to strike the ball with a downward blow, rather than "scooping" it. In order to do this, you must keep the back of your left hand leading the clubhead through impact. Here's a way to check that your left hand always leads: Hold the club along with an additional long, thin stick, such as a golf shaft or a yardstick. At address the top of this stick should extend well above the grip, and to the left of your left hip. Now make your chipping stroke. The stick should stay in front of your hip at and beyond impact. If it brushes your hip, it means your left wrist has "cupped" and you've scooped the shot.

MASTER·STROKES

Read The Lie Before You Chip

A chip shot from a short distance off the green should loft the ball just onto the green, then let it run to the hole. You need to take the right-lofted club to land the ball on the green, and to do this, you must also know how the lie will affect the shot.

If the ball is lying nicely on fairway grass, say, eight feet off the green and 40 feet from the hole, an 8-iron might give you the right loft and roll. But if the shot is the same distance with the ball in snarly rough, remember that the ball will come out lower and with less backspin. You'll need to play this chip with a more-lofted club, either a pitching wedge or a sand wedge.

50°

MASTER·STROKES

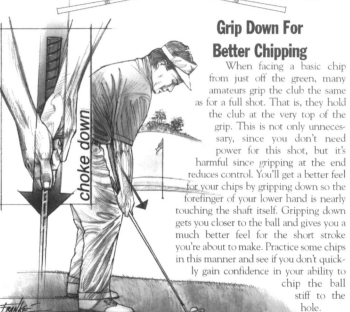

Grip Down For Better Chipping

When facing a basic chip from just off the green, many amateurs grip the club the same as for a full shot. That is, they hold the club at the very top of the grip. This is not only unnecessary, since you don't need power for this shot, but it's harmful since gripping at the end reduces control. You'll get a better feel for your chips by gripping down so the forefinger of your lower hand is nearly touching the shaft itself. Gripping down gets you closer to the ball and gives you a much better feel for the short stroke you're about to make. Practice some chips in this manner and see if you don't quickly gain confidence in your ability to chip the ball stiff to the hole.

choke down

FRANKIE

MASTER·STROKES

Chip Under The Bench

Many golfers chip poorly because they try to "lift" the ball up, and contact the ground before the ball. In the correct chipping action, the hands lead the clubhead down and through so you strike the ball with a crisp, descending blow. This produces a low, controlled shot that lands just on the green and then rolls to the hole.

Here's a drill to help your chipping stroke. Take an 8-iron and a ball. Set a workbench or picnic bench eight feet in front of you. Then hit a chip toward it. Your goal is to chip the ball under the bench, not over it. To do this you must emphasize the hands-ahead contact which helps you contact the ball solidly and keep it low.

MASTER STROKES

When To Use The Texas Wedge

Chips from firm ground or hardpan call for more precision than chips from soft fairway turf. With no cushion under the ball, it's easier to hit behind it and leave it way short. This is particularly true if you're playing a lofted chip.

When playing from hard, dry, fairly level ground around the green, the putter, also known as the "Texas Wedge," is usually the best choice. You can reasonably use the putter from up to 20 yards off the putting surface. Just read the speed and break of this shot as you would a long putt, for that's really what it is. You'll find chips played with your Texas Wedge finishing much closer to the hole on average.

MASTER STROKES

"Shortest" Chip Gives Best Results

You're six feet off the green and at least 60 feet from the hole. Many golfers will take a wedge and hit a shot that carries much of the distance to the hole on the fly. It's much harder to judge the shot playing it this way. Instead, simplify your chips. Figure out what club you need to loft the ball just three feet onto the putting surface, then give the ball enough run to just reach the hole. This might be a 6-, 7- or 8-iron. Now all you have to do is hit a chip that carries a total of nine feet in the air to the spot you've chosen just onto the green. Hitting the "shortest" possible chip takes the guesswork out and will allow you to play these shots with your old confidence.

3'

6'

MASTER STROKES

Use Enough Loft On Greenside Chips

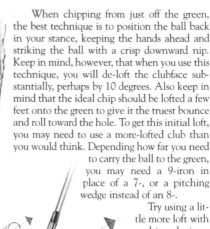

When chipping from just off the green, the best technique is to position the ball back in your stance, keeping the hands ahead and striking the ball with a crisp downward nip. Keep in mind, however, that when you use this technique, you will de-loft the clubface substantially, perhaps by 10 degrees. Also keep in mind that the ideal chip should be lofted a few feet onto the green to give it the truest bounce and roll toward the hole. To get this initial loft, you may need to use a more-lofted club than you would think. Depending how far you need to carry the ball to the green, you may need a 9-iron in place of a 7-, or a pitching wedge instead of an 8-.

Try using a little more loft with this technique. You'll like the results.

MASTER·STROKES

Fairway Wood Chip

It's possible you can improve your chipping from just off the green by hitting these little shots with a 5-wood. This works well when your ball is just barely into the light rough, where you can't use the putter because the ball may hop out erratically. Instead, use a lofted fairway wood and simply make a normal, smooth putting stroke with it. The slight loft on the club serves to get the ball just up and out of the light rough, then set it onto the fringe rolling smoothly. With a little practice, you'll find you can consistently roll the ball close.

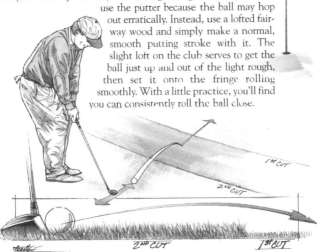

1ST CUT

2ND CUT

2ND CUT

1ST CUT

MASTER·STROKES

Chip Over Or Short Of Slopes

On many courses you'll encounter greens with two levels separated by a severe slope. You may face a chip from the lower level to a flag on the upper level. When planning this tricky shot, make one of two choices: 1. Take a less-lofted club (6- or 7-iron) and hit a running shot that lands just on the green and runs up and over the slope. 2. If there's plenty of room on the upper level between the slope and the flag, you can hit a pitch with a sand or lob wedge that carries the up-slope yet stops near the hole. But never plan a shot that lands the ball into the slope itself. This makes it very difficult to judge how much the ball will roll after landing; often it will roll back down the slope, leaving a long, difficult putt.

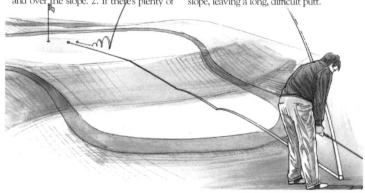

MASTER·STROKES

Keep Short Game Basic In Early Season

As a new season gets underway, keep in mind that course conditions may not be quite as pure as in later spring. There may be a number of bare spots or the grass may be thin, so there's not much cushion underneath the ball. This can make your short game shots particularly hazardous. So in early season, play the percentages with your short game. Avoid trying high lob shots, which require you to slip the clubface of a lofted wedge perfectly underneath the ball. Instead, when the lies are tight, play more basic chip shots using slightly less lofted clubs and allowing the ball to run more. By simplifying your short game selections, you'll fare better in the early going.

Yes

No

MASTER·STROKES

Chip Into Slope When Lie Is Tight

You've missed the green and your ball has rolled down a slope away from the green. The flag is located fairly close to your side, so you don't have much room to stop the ball. Your first thought is to play a high, soft lob shot. However, if your lie is tight with little or no cushion under the ball, a lob shot is very risky. Instead, a low chip into the bank in front of you is the percentage shot. Select a club that, with your normal chipping setup and swing, will carry the ball halfway up the slope, and give it enough momentum to climb the rest of the way up and onto the green. (This will most often be a 5-, 6-, or 7-iron.) The into-the-slope chip is very much a "feel" shot, so practice it on the course when the opportunity arises.

MASTER·STROKES

Pitch Like You'd Toss

When you are facing a short pitch over sand or rough, use your imagination. Visualize tossing the ball with your hand on the trajectory you'd need to stop it near the hole. If the flag is tucked tight to your side, you would have to toss the ball high and land it softly just onto the green. To reproduce this flight you'd need to use your most lofted wedge. However, say the hole is on the other side of the green so you have plenty of green to work with. Here, you'd want to toss the ball on a lower trajectory, again landing it just onto the green and letting it run the rest of the way. For this shot, select a lower-lofted club that will duplicate this imaginary "toss."

MASTER·STROKES

Play The Pitch And Run

Most golfers, when faced with shots of 50-80 yards, automatically reach for the sand or lob wedge and play a high, soft pitch. This isn't always the best shot choice. If the flag is on the back half of the green so you have plenty of room to land the ball, play the pitch and run instead. This shot uses most of the green, landing the ball on the front and letting it run to the hole. Depending on the total yardage and the amount of green in front of the hole, you might play it with a 9-iron or pitching wedge. Address the ball in the middle of your stance, hands slightly ahead. This will help you contact the ball before the bottom of your swing for clean, solid contact. With practice, you'll find it easier to hit the pitch and run pin-high and in one-putt range.

YES

MASTER·STROKES

Imagine A Tree On Short Lob Shots

How can you play a soft lob to carry over water, sand or rough and stop it near a tight pin? Your best weapon is your imagination. Visualize a tall tree growing between ball and hole, so high that any shot getting over it would drop down on a steep parabola close to the hole. Next, imagine the setup and swing needed to flop the ball over the tree—weight more on your rear foot, ball more forward in your stance, clubface laid back for more loft, and a smooth, lazy swing action that slides your wedge under the ball at impact.

MASTER·STROKES

Dead Hands With The Lob Wedge

The lob wedge is the most lofted club in the bag (about 60 degrees of loft). It's a tremendous tool when you need to hit a high, soft pitch shot. When using the lob wedge, remember that the loft on the clubface alone will provide all the height you need; you don't have to use a "handsy" action at impact to flip the ball up. Instead, concentrate on making a slow, smooth arm swing on all lob shots from normal lies, keeping your hands quiet or "dead" through the impact zone. Such a "dead hands" swing, along with a steady head, allows you the best chance to deliver the lofted clubface cleanly to the ball for consistent results.

MASTER·STROKES

Aim Pitches At Top Of Flag

When faced with a short pitch that must be hit high and softly, most amateurs leave the shot short. When you're focusing on sliding a lofted wedge under the ball to get it up quickly, most of the energy imparted by the club is used to shoot the ball upward, not forward. So it's easy to leave the shot short of the flag, if not the entire green.

A tip: When visualizing short pitch shots, aim for the top of the flagstick. A shot that would hit the top of the flagstick would, of course, land the ball slightly past the hole. You don't want this, but aiming for the top of the flag will offset the tendency to "baby" the shot. So, you'll at least get the ball to reach the hole.

MASTER STROKES

The Hooded Sand Wedge Pitch

There will be times when you need to hit a short pitch to a tightly-placed pin, but the wind is firmly against you. A soft pitch will get eaten up by the wind. Here, the hooded sand wedge pitch is a real weapon. Position the ball back of center in a narrow, slightly open stance. Place most of your weight on your left foot with hands 3 to 4 inches ahead of the ball. This "hoods" the club-face, reducing loft.

Swing the club back on an upright arc. Use mostly your arms, with little weight shift. Swing back down on the same steep arc. The ball will start off with a lower-than-normal flight to fight the wind. However, it will be loaded with backspin so that when it lands, it will take one small hop, and then stop dead.

MASTER·STROKES

Use the Green On Pitch Shots

Many amateurs, when facing a pitch to a green with the pin near the back, play the wrong type of approach. They try to hit a high lob all the way to the hole, then stop it dead. Too often they come up way short; sometimes, when the green is hard, the ball can bound over into trouble.

When you have plenty of green to work with, use it. Plan a lower shot, a pitch-and-run with a 9-iron, pitching wedge or "gap" wedge. You want the shot to carry to the front half of the green, so you'll get a true first bounce, and then release back to the hole. You'll find it much easier to judge the total distance this way rather than by the "all carry" route.

NO

Yes

MASTER·STROKES

Read the Lie Before You Lob

On courses with lots of mounding around the greens, you'll face some recovery shots where a high, soft lob shot is ideal to get the ball close. However, before deciding to play this shot, check the lie closely. In order to play a soft lob, you must be able to slip the clubface of your most lofted club under the ball rather than hitting down on it. And, you must have a good cushion between the bottom of the ball and the turf. If the ball is lying tight to the ground, the degree of precision needed to strike the shot correctly is so high that playing the lob is not worth the risk. So, make sure the ball is sitting "up" before committing to the lob shot.

TOO TIGHT   SITTING "UP"

MASTER·STROKES

Play "Sand" Shot From Greenside Rough

Occasionally your ball will find deep greenside rough, with the pin close so you don't have much room to stop the shot. In these situations, play the shot like a greenside bunker shot. Address the ball with the blade of your sand wedge open or "laid back." Aim for a spot a full 2 inches behind the ball. Cock your wrists quickly on the backswing to create a steep arc, then bring the club down at your spot behind the ball, rather than the ball itself. The ball will pop up and out softly and land with little roll. Practice to determine the force of swing needed for various distances, and soon this recovery method will be second nature.

Section 8:
SAND PLAY

Greenside sand shots terrify many amateurs. This is really a shame, because the basic greenside sand shot is one of the easiest shots in golf! Why? You'll see when you read the advice on the basic sand shot, that there is actually a larger margin of error here than on other shots. That's because you are contacting the sand behind the ball, rather than precisely striking the back of the ball itself.

That said, there are a number of complications to the basic sand shot that you'll run into when you're out on the course—buried lies, downhill lies, uphill lies, unusual sand textures, and more. What else would you expect? After all, a sand trap is a hazard! After reading this section, you should be well prepared to successfully deal with all sand play situations.

Section 8:

CONTENTS

MASTER·STROKES

The Dollar Bill Sand Shot

Are you psyched out by greenside sand shots? Afraid of "scalping" the ball over the green or flubbing it and leaving it in the bunker? Here's a mental image that can help you overcome your fear: Imagine that the ball in the bunker is resting on the center of a dollar bill. Address the ball with the blade of your sand wedge "laid back" so it has added loft. Next, ignore the ball as you swing. Concentrate instead on sliding the wedge into the sand and slapping that "dollar bill" out on a thin layer of sand. If you do this, the ball will pop up and out softly onto the green, and soon your fear of the greenside sand shot will be history.

FACE
OPEN

MASTER·STROKES

Sand Depth Affects Shot Distance

firm sand

soft sand

You face a medium-length greenside sand shot, where you must carry the ball 30 feet to the green and another 30 feet to the hole. The texture of the sand can make a big difference in how much force you must use.

As you walk into the bunker and assume your stance, pay close attention to the depth of the sand. Is it soft, or is it so shallow that you feel the hard base beneath the sand? If you can feel the base, your sand wedge will "bounce" more: The ball will come out lower and carry farther, so you'll need less swing force. If the sand is deep, you'll need a bigger swing to carry the ball well onto the green. Practice to get a feel for the amount of force needed from various sand textures.

MASTER·STROKES

Upright Swing From Bunkers

Most amateurs struggle from greenside bunkers. A common flaw is to swing the sand wedge on a plane that's too "flat." This flat approach angle causes the club's sole to catch the sand too early. The most common result is that the sole bounces off the sand and then skulls the ball, sending it over the green.

Cock your wrists early on the backswing for sand shots. This forces the clubhead to move up on a steeper, or more upright, path. Then simply swing down on the same fairly steep path. This makes it much easier to hit your "target spot" in the sand a couple of inches behind the ball, with enough downward force so that the leading edge works under the ball, popping it nicely up and out.

No

Yes

MASTER·STROKES

Adjustments For Buried Lie

Occasionally your ball will be buried in the face of a bunker, and it looks like you'll need so much brute force there's no chance to get it out in one shot. Here are two tips to help you escape more easily than you'd think: 1. Use a pitching wedge, not a sand wedge. The sharper leading edge will cut into the sand and get under the ball better; 2. Address the ball with a square clubface as opposed to the open clubface you'd use from a good lie in the sand. This too helps the club dig deeper.

Hit down sharply one-and-a-half inches behind the ball and don't worry about a follow-through. You'll be surprised at how easily the ball pops out.

MASTER·STROKES

Adjust Clubface for Sand Depth

On greenside bunker shots, knowing whether the sand is deep or shallow is important in determining how to set up to play the shot successfully. As you step into your address, gauge the depth of the sand as you wiggle your feet into it. If the sand is shallow and hard, the clubhead will have a tendency to bounce off the surface behind the ball so you skull the shot. So from hard sand, square the face of your sand wedge so that it will dig in enough to get underneath the ball.

Conversely, if the sand feels very soft and fluffy, you want the clubhead to slide rather than dig. In this situation, open the blade wide. This allows the trailing lower edge of the sand wedge flange to act as a rudder, skimming the club just under the surface.

DIG!

firm

OPEN

SLIDE

soft

MASTER·STROKES

When To Chip From Bunkers

The long greenside bunker shot (25 to 50 yards) is tough. You need lots of force to "blast" the ball all the way to the hole.

When the conditions permit, chip it. You need a good clean lie in a bunker with a fairly low lip. Take an 8-iron, 9-iron or pitching wedge (lower loft for more run, more left for less run). Position the ball back of center in a narrow stance, and choke well down on the grip for better control. Swing with your arms, keeping head and body still, and concentrate on meeting the ball first. It will come out low, then skip and roll all the way to the flag. With practice, the bunker chip can be a great weapon!

choke down

ball back of center

MASTER STROKES

Adjustments For Uphill Sand Shot

Your ball may come to rest on an upslope near the front of a greenside bunker. The uphill bunker shot is somewhat simpler than a downhill shot, but can still cause problems. It's easy to pop the ball high and leave it well short. Or, you can skull the ball, line-driving it over the green.

To play the shot successfully, do the following: **1.** Set your feet securely with weight evenly balanced and shoulders parallel to the sand's slope. This keeps you from digging too deep into the sand. **2.** Position the ball no farther forward in your stance than opposite inside of left heel. **3.** Aim to hit the sand a fraction closer to the ball than normal—say, 2 inches behind instead of 2 1/2. **4.** Swing normally. If you can't fly the ball to the hole using a sand wedge, use a gap or pitching wedge instead.

gap wedge

2"

MASTER STROKES

Adjustments For Downhill Bunker Shot

The biggest tendency on downhill bunker shots is to hit the ball itself rather than contacting only the sand behind it, so that you skull the shot over the green. There are two adjustments to make. First, aim to hit a spot in the sand farther behind the ball than normal—since the sand is sloping down, you must hit a spot farther back so the flange of your sand wedge can work under the base of the ball. So instead of two inches behind, aim for a spot three to four inches behind the ball. Next, don't open the blade of your sand wedge quite as much as from a flat lie. This also will help the flange to dig rather than bounce off the sand. Remember finally that the ball will come out lower and roll farther.

open face

MASTER·STROKES

"Nip" Your Sand Shots

Many golfers believe that they must make a big "blast" when playing greenside sand shots. When your club hits the sand too far behind the ball and/or digs too deeply, it requires tremendous strength to keep the clubhead moving so that the ball gets out.

Instead of thinking "blast" from greenside bunkers, start thinking "nip." Assuming the lie is good, keep the clubface open, then simply try to nip a very shallow cut of sand out from under the ball. The less sand you can take, the less force you'll need. Practice this method and you'll see that getting the ball on the green from bunkers is much less strenuous than you'd think.

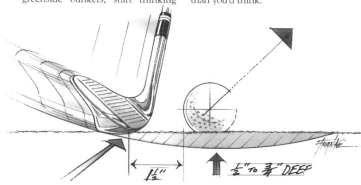

$1\frac{1}{2}$" $\frac{1}{2}$" to $\frac{3}{4}$" DEEP

MASTER·STROKES

"Long"

"Medium"

"Short"

Adjust Follow-Through
On Sand Shots

The safest way for amateurs to play greenside sand shots of different lengths is to use the same basic swing technique and try to hit the same distance behind the ball. Then, adjust the force needed for various distances.

To adjust your swing force for short or long sand shots, visualize three different follow-throughs: For very short greenside shots, your hands should finish just below your waist; for medium-length shots (40-60 feet), let your hands reach chest height; and when you face a long sand shots of over 60 feet, make sure to swing your arms through to a point above your shoulders.

MASTER·STROKES

Putt From the Trap

You can save strokes by being alert to situations in sand traps where the lie is good, the sand is fairly flat and there is very little lip. In such cases, you can often do well by putting the ball out.

Say the lip of the trap is 15 feet away, the edge of the green 25 feet away and the distance to the flagstick is 60 feet. Visualize the force you would need to putt the ball 60 feet; then add about 50 percent more force to this imagined stroke, since more energy will be needed to start the ball through the sand and greenside fringe. Keep your stroke long, slow and relatively level and your head still. You'll putt the ball out every time, and often get it to finish close.

MASTER·STROKES

Solving The Long Bunker Shot

Occasionally you'll find a bunker a short distance from the green, leaving you 30-50 yards to the hole. For such a long sand shot, you can't use your standard greenside sand technique and still get the ball to the hole. Here's how to adjust: Instead of your sand wedge, select a 9-iron or pitching wedge. Aim more "square" to the target than for a short sand shot. Dig in your feet just slightly—if you dig in too deeply, you'll hit too far behind the ball. Try to contact the sand a bit closer to the ball than for a greenside sand shot, say, 2 inches behind the ball instead of 2-1/2 inches. Swing normally, and follow through fully. Practice with both the 9 iron and pitching wedge to get a feel for the distances you can cover with each club.

9 IRON

2"

NOT TOO DEEP

FRANKS

CLOSE TO SQUARE

Section 9:
PUTTING

Putting is the most important part of the game of golf. For the average amateur who shoots a score in the 90s for 18 holes, some 40 percent of their strokes will be putts! So, it pays to put a substantial portion of your time and concentration into this segment of the game.

The section that follows will examine much more than how to develop a consistent putting stroke. There are myriad other areas that are a part of being, or becoming, a good putter. These include topics such as setting up to the ball correctly; styles of putting grips; reading the green's surface both for its speed and its slope; drills to enhance solid contact; adjustments that will help you on short putts; and developing a rock-solid putting routine that helps build confidence. Consider the suggestions made herein, select the ones that you believe will best aid any deficiencies you might have, and you will gradually begin to see more putts drop.

Section 9:
CONTENTS

MASTER STROKES

Firm Up Putting Routine

It's easy to get nervous over putts, particularly short to middle distance putts you need to hole to score well. A nervous stroke usually results.

The best way to make a "nerveless" stroke is to make it part of a routine. It's not too important what movements you make. It is important to set a pre-stroke routine that flows smoothly into the stroke itself. For example, you might set the blade behind the ball, look from ball to hole once or twice, and make a slight forward press of your hands toward the target. The key is to make these movements the same way every time, then immediately continue with the stroke itself. Developing a rock-solid routine will make the putting stroke "automatic"— and you more confident.

MASTER·STROKES

Hands Beneath Shoulders

Many golfers have trouble keeping the putter moving along the target line. In most cases, the blade moves along a path that "curves" to the inside on the backstroke, and then inside again on the follow-through. This leads to inconsistency in starting the ball on the correct line.

Here's a setup tip that really helps: At address, make sure your hands are directly beneath your shoulder sockets. Then, if you make a desirable back-and-through stroke with your shoulders, your hands will move back and forth along a straight line. And if your hands move along a straight line, so will the putter! See if this setup tip doesn't automatically improve your stroke.

MASTER·STROKES

Head In Vise
For Precise Putting

If you move your head as you stroke any putt, the odds of your making that putt go down. When the head moves, the upper body and arms must move with it. This in turn means that the blade of the putter will never quite impact the ball precisely as you had planned. It doesn't take much head movement to throw the blade off enough to affect the path of the ball by an inch or two—the difference between a make and a miss.

As you settle in over the ball, imagine a large vise being lightly tightened against your temples, fixing your head's position in space. Make your stroke with your head locked in by that vise, never looking up until the ball is long gone. A truer roll will result.

MASTER STROKES

Low Back, Low Through

In making the putting stroke, it always helps to remember to keep the putter blade low to the ground throughout the stroke. By deciding in advance to keep the blade low, you will make a stroking action controlled by your arms rather than by your wrists and hands. You will make a more consistent stroke by using your arms. Also, by keeping the putterhead low, it means you'll give the ball a nice level hit with the putter blade, rather than a downward, "chopping" type of stroke. Result: The ball gets off to a much smoother roll and has a better chance of staying on the intended line.

MASTER·STROKES

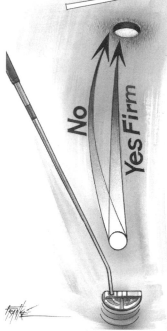

No / Yes Firm

Take Break Out of Short Putts

Oftentimes when you face a slick three-footer that has some break, the tendency is to try to read the break perfectly and "curl" the ball in. This works for some, but it requires great judgment and touch. However, if you stroke the putt a bit more firmly, you will take most of the break out of it. Most times on the short ones, if you resolve to make a firm stroke, you can aim "inside the hole." When the ball rolls with more speed on a putt this short, it won't have time to break. Take a slightly firmer approach to the short curlers, and you'll make more of them.

MASTER STROKES

The Solid Contact Putting Drill

There is nothing you can do in putting that will help you more than to contact the ball perfectly squarely, so that it leaves the putterface rolling end-over-end immediately. Here's a little-known practice tip: Take a nickel and stand it up edgewise on your kitchen linoleum or a wooden floor. Then make your stroke for about a 10-foot putt, striking the nickel squarely on its back edge so that it rolls forward just like a wheel. If you can get to the point where you can make the nickel "roll" consistently, you'll know that you'll be rolling the golf ball purely, too.

MASTER·STROKES

Does Putting Grip Differ?

Should you putt with the same grip that you use for full shots? There's no rule against this, however, most better golfers opt for a different grip when putting. One of the most popular is the reverse overlap. In this grip, all of the fingers of the right hand are on the grip. Meanwhile, the index finger of the left hand overlaps the fingers of the right hand, either pointing down the grip or curling around the fingers somewhat as shown. You'll find that this grip gives you a better feel of the club with your right hand, allowing you to push the putter head down the target line with increased accuracy and feel for distance.

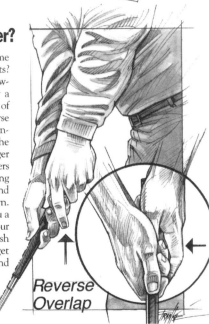

Reverse Overlap

MASTER·STROKES

Make Handle Lead Blade

Many amateurs hit poor putts because the left or lead wrist breaks down, with the putterhead moving ahead of the hands at impact. The clubface hits the ball while moving upward, so contact is not as solid; and the clubface also closes slightly so the tendency is to miss left.

A tip for solid putting: Keep the handle one to two inches ahead of the blade through and past impact. Set up with the handle leading the clubhead and the left wrist flat, then keep the left wrist in that flat position throughout the stroke. Practice this setup and stroke as it may feel a bit awkward at first. The result will be solid, level contact which produces a better roll, with the clubface staying right on the line.

**1"-2"
ahead**

MASTER·STROKES

Eyes Over the Ball

There are a number of theories on why older golfers don't putt as well as in their younger days. One is that their vision has changed and they don't "see the line" as well. Here's a tip that can help: Practice setting up to putts so that your eyes are directly over the ball. You can check this by setting up with a ruler dangling downward from between your eyes. Does the end of the ruler point directly to the ball? Most golfers will have their eyes set inside the line of putt; a minority have their eyes over a line outside the ball. In either case, you don't have a "right angle" between your eyes, the ball and the target line. Work on getting your eyes over the ball. With practice, you'll gain confidence in getting the ball started on target.

MASTER STROKES

Sink Every Putt

You may have heard the advice that on long putts, your goal should be to "lag" the ball within a three-foot circle of the hole. The notion is that this will somehow help you determine the correct speed, which in turn will reduce three-putts.

A better approach, though, is to simply try to sink every putt, no matter what the distance. Why shouldn't you? By doing all you can to sink putts in the 30-50 foot range as well as the short ones, you will automatically tune in to the optimum speed and line that will give the ball the best chance to drop. So, go ahead and try to sink every putt. The end result will be sharper overall putting.

MASTER STROKES

Keep Stroke Tempo Smooth

Many golfers tend to make "quick" or "nervous" strokes, leading to erratic results on the greens. You can improve your stroke by keeping it as smooth as possible from start to finish. Strive to make the stroke the same length going back as it is going through, and keep the tempo identical from start to finish. Every time you putt, imagine that there's a metronome next to your ball. Count a smooth "One" for your backstroke and "Two" for your downstroke, and soon you'll be rolling the ball with confidence.

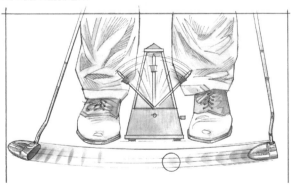

MASTER·STROKES

Read the Grain

On many putting surfaces, particularly Bermuda greens in warm climates, the grass leans in one direction. Such grass is said to have "grain," and grain is a factor in your overall read of the putt.

To determine the grain, look directly down towards the cup. If on one side the grass looks ruffled while the opposite side appears clean-cut, the grain is growing from the ruffled side toward the clean side. So if you are putting with the ruffled side at the rear of the cup, the putt is into the grain and you must stroke more firmly; if the clean side is at the rear, you are putting "with" the grain and it will roll a bit farther than normal. If the ruffled grass is on either side of the cup, plan for the putt to break away from that side a little more than you'd think.

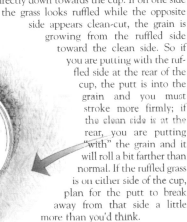

with grain

against grain

MASTER·STROKES

Widen Putting Stance On Windy Days

When putting, even the slightest body movement during the stroke can alter the angle of the putter face enough to send the putt off line. And it's harder than you think to stay perfectly still if you're playing in windy conditions.

Here's a good tip. When a firm breeze is blowing, widen your putting stance about six to eight inches. A wider base is more stable and will also put you a little closer to the ground, so that you're more likely to stay still throughout the stroke.

More online putts will result, even in the wind.

MASTER·STROKES

Marry Face Angle And Stroke Path

In order to hit pure putts, you must strike the ball perfectly squarely, just as on a full shot. The putterhead must move directly along the intended starting line while the putterface is square to the intended target. Amateurs' most common error is to pull the putter from outside-in, while (without realizing it) keeping the putterface slightly open to compensate. While this may work to some degree, it will never be as consistent as is marrying a square stroke path with a

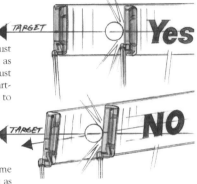

square clubface. A tip: Practice your stroke between two rulers that are on your target line to make sure your stroke path is square. Then, use the ruler marks to check that the putterface is aligned square to your target. More consistent putting will result.

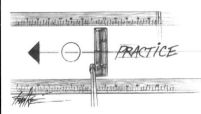

MASTER·STROKES

Double-Breaker Putts

Sometimes on longer putts you will face a situation where the ball rolls over terrain that breaks first one way, then the other. How can you judge the line accurately?

Say the putt is 35 feet. The first 15 feet breaks right-to-left, then, after flattening out for about five feet, the remaining 15 feet breaks left-to-right. In this case you might assume the two breaks will cancel each other out, so you should start the ball straight at the hole. Keep in mind, however, that the ball will break more as it slows down, in this case meaning it will break more to the right as it approaches the hole. So, start the putt slightly left of the hole to allow for this.

15'

LESS SPEED
MORE BREAK

15'

MORE SPEED
LESS BREAK

RANKE

MASTER·STROKES

Back of Cup On Slow Putts

Often, at the beginning of the golf season, the greens will be slow—there's lots of rain, the ground stays moist, and the grass grows quickly. So there's a tendency to leave putts short, and also to play too much break. On slow greens and particularly on the shorter putts, be aggressive. Play a bit less break than you would if the greens were quicker, and aim to hit the back of the cup with your putt. Imagine that there's a tack that's pushed part way into the back lip of the hole. Try to roll the ball firmly enough so that it hits the tack and pushes it all the way in. With this firmer stroke, you'll find you can sink a lot of putts on slow greens.

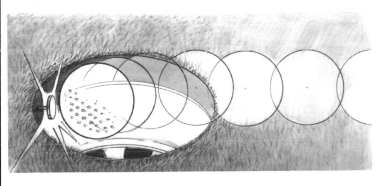

MASTER·STROKES

Focus On Starting Line

On shorter breaking putts, there's a strong tendency to move the putter along a line toward the hole, rather than along the intended starting line. The result is a missed putt to the "low" side.

Here's a tip to help: Say you're facing a 10-foot putt that you think will break 12 inches to the right. Align the putter toward an imaginary hole just three feet away. The center of this hole is actually along the line you need to roll the ball on your "real" putt. Once you're perfectly aligned, focus on rolling your three-footer right in the middle, and you'll make the breaking 10-footer as well!

MASTER·STROKES

"Label" Your Putts

Most golfers don't realize it, but they may miss more putts through poor aim than because of an errant stroke. To help get your stroke on-line, do the following: After you've determined the starting line of the putt, place your ball so that the label lies directly along that line. Then, simply set your putter blade down so that it is at a perfect right angle to the ball's label. You'll know you're lined up where you want to be, so go ahead and stroke it with confidence.

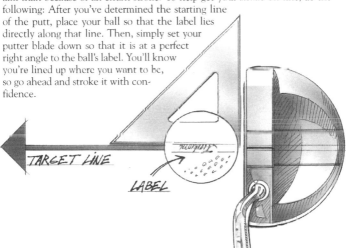

TARGET LINE

LABEL

MASTER·STROKES

Left Hand Low

One of the frustrating facts for many veteran golfers is that they don't sink as many putts as in years past, particularly "testers" from four to eight feet. If you're near the point of despair using a conventional putting setup, consider the "left hand low" method. This is where (for a right-handed player) you set your left hand beneath the right on the putter grip. The advantage of this setup is that the back of your left hand, wrist and forearm are in nearly a straight-line position at address, and it's nearly impossible for the left wrist to "break" during the stroke. The result is a stroke which stays more level and delivers a solid hit for a truer roll and more sunk putts.

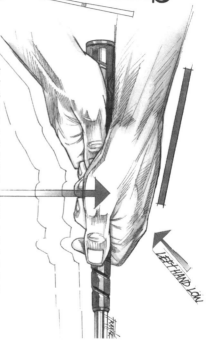

LEFT HAND LOW

MASTER STROKES

Marry Line To Speed

When reading a putt, keep in mind that the green's speed will greatly affect the amount of break. Say you have a 25-footer with a right-to-left break. If the green is slow, the ball will break less than normal. That's because you must hit the putt with more force, so it holds its line for a longer distance. Also, the longer grass blades will keep the ball from breaking much as it slows down. On a very fast green the putt will break much more—since you must strike the ball more softly, it will not have as much forward impetus and the slope will begin to affect it earlier. Also, the short grass blades will offer less resistance to the ball's weight as it slows near the hole. So, always factor the speed of the putt into the amount of break.

SLOW LINE

FAST LINE

MASTER·STROKES

Shoulders Square To Starting Line

On big breaking putts, it's sometimes difficult to get the ball started on the right line. Most amateurs miss to the "low" side because they haven't started the ball on a line that's high enough to take the break into full account.

It will help greatly on breaking putts if you align your shoulders square to the starting line of the putt. Say the putt breaks three feet to the left. Align your shoulders squarely to a line that starts 3 feet to the right of the hole, rather than aligning at the hole itself. With your shoulders square to the starting line of putt, you can now make a natural stroking motion, while getting the putt started on the correct line.

3'

FRANKE

MASTER·STROKES

Putt Decisively!

An easy trap for golfers to fall into is to try to "wish" the ball into the hole—particularly on putts under 10 feet that you know you should make a high percentage of. Even if you do sometimes lack confidence from this distance, if you want to remain a good putter, you must force yourself to be decisive. Determine your line, line up the putter, set up to the ball and stroke it for the back of the cup. Don't dawdle over the ball and give doubts time to creep in. If you practice a set, decisive pattern of lining up and firmly stroking your putts, and stick with it on the course, you'll be the best putter you can be.

MASTER STROKES

Make A Slow-Motion Stroke

Most golfers, even some pros, make a putting stroke that's quicker and "handsier" than it should be. This leads to poor contact, poor clubface alignment and, of course, missed putts.

Try this next time you play: Read and set up to each putt as normally. Then try to make a stroke that's literally in slow motion. Imagine that you're standing in ankle-deep water, so that you're forced to move the clubhead very slowly both back from and through the ball. You may notice immediately that you're making smooth, level contact and the ball starts rolling very smoothly. Keep stroking in slow motion and many more putts will fall.

SLOW

Master Strokes

"On Path" On Short Putts

On longer putts, a normal stroke is one where the path of the putter moves slightly inside the target line on both the backstroke and follow-through. However, on short putts of five feet or less, you need only move the blade a few inches back and through. On the short testers, try moving the putter straight back from and through the ball, while keeping the putter blade perfectly square to your target line throughout the stroke. Keep your head very still and you'll make just about every one of them.

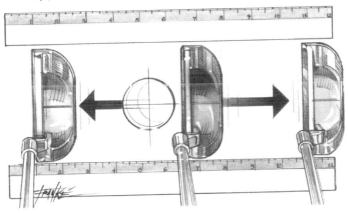

MASTER·STROKES

"Multiply" Stroke on Long Putts

On putts of 40 feet and longer, it's difficult to correctly gauge the force of the stroke you'll need. Here's a mental gimmick that really helps: Walk from the hole to a point that's halfway along the line back to your ball (25 feet for a 50-footer). From this spot, take a practice stroke of the length needed for this distance. Try to retain the feel of this stroke as you go back to the ball. Then, simply multiply the force of the stroke by two to give you the amount of power you need for your "real" stroke.

By dividing these lengthy putts in half and "feeling" the distance for each half, you get a much better sense of the force you'll need to lag the long ones close.

MASTER·STROKES

Learn From Missed Putts

Here's a tip to help you make more second putts: Watch your first putts more carefully!

Sometimes when you have a long first putt you'll hit it a shade too hard, so the ball runs a few feet past. As the ball reaches the hole and slides by, observe its path closely. Any break that occurs from the time it passes the hole until it stops, is what will happen in reverse when you hit your second putt. So you will always have a clear idea of how your comeback putt will break. You should also use this tip whenever you hit a chip from off the green, observing the ball's path if it rolls past the hole.

TAKE
NOTE.

MASTER·STROKES

Firm Uphill, Soft Downhill

On sloping greens, adjust your approach to uphill and downhill putts. Many amateurs fail to hit uphill putts hard enough. They leave the ball short, or miss because they don't hit it firmly enough to hold the intended line. On the other hand, golfers may hit downhill putts too firmly, so if the putt misses it zips well past.

On uphill putts, strike firmly enough so that the ball hits the back of the cup lightly before dropping in. Even if you miss, since it's rolling uphill the ball will stop just past. On downhillers, try to make the ball drop over the front lip without touching the back of the hole. This way, should you miss, the ball will still stop within tap-in distance.

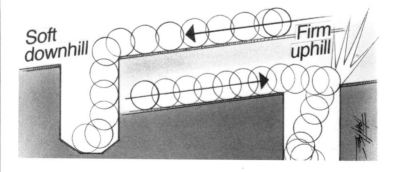

Soft downhill

Firm uphill

MASTER·STROKES

"Read" As Important As Stroke

How often have you stroked a putt and everything felt right, yet the ball never touched the hole? If so, don't assume your stroke was faulty. Your "read" might have been the culprit.

Work on your green-reading on various putts on the practice green. Look closely at the contours, especially those nearest the hole. Factor in the speed of the green — more speed equals more total break. Finally, keep in mind that everyone's sight changes as they age. Your read — and your putting — are sure to benefit if your corrective vision prescription is up to date and sharp for both near and far objects.

MASTER·STROKES

Wind Can Affect Putts

Did you ever stop to think that your putts can be influenced by the wind? When the wind is blowing firmly, it will make a definite difference, particularly on dry greens in open settings, and especially if they're elevated.

Say you face a long downhiller, and the wind's blowing with your line of putt. Even though you think you've judged the speed carefully, after your stroke, you watch the ball trickle six, eight, even 10 feet past the cup. If you're putting into the wind, you may notice the ball pulls up a little short; if the wind is blowing strongly across the line, it will make the ball turn slightly in that direction. So remember to factor any significant wind into your read of the putt.

MASTER·STROKES

More Speed = More Break

A putt from the same position can require a different "read" at different times. Say you face a putt that usually breaks six inches to the right. On this occasion, you're playing on a weekend morning right after the greens have been cut, and they're quick. Because you must stroke softly, the ball will roll with less momentum and therefore it's more susceptible to gravity. The putt may now break eight to nine inches instead of six. Conversely, if the greens haven't been cut and rain has made the greens moist, you must hit the putt harder than normal. The ball will break less, perhaps three inches. So, figure the current state of the green, as well as its slope, into your read.

MASTER·STROKES

When To Change Putters

Everyone falls into a putting slump from time to time. Very often, golfers will decide that their club is the problem. They'll change putters frequently, perhaps even for every round, trying to find one that has the "magic."

If you've been struggling, it's not a bad idea to change to a new putter for a few rounds. This may give you a temporary boost in confidence. But don't use different putters as a crutch. Remember that you had good luck with your old putter before, so there's certainly nothing wrong with it. Take a careful look at your setup and stroke mechanics on the practice green. Chances are you'll find a flaw. Once you repair the flaw, you'll see that your old putter can sink plenty of putts for you!

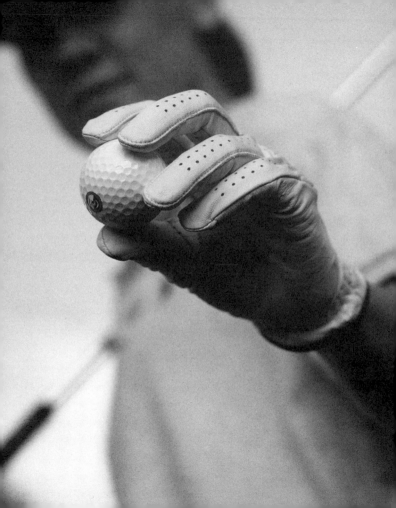

PLAYING STRATEGY

Ask any amateur who's going out for a round, what their "game plan" is for the day's play. You'd be likely to receive some funny looks, or at least some blank stares. The fact is, most amateurs don't have a game plan. Strategy of play is, at best, an afterthought, something that they worry about only after they have hit a poorly struck or poorly thought-out shot that puts them in big trouble.

Once you have reached a moderate to proficient skill level so that you can keep the ball reasonably well within the field of play, points of strategy become more and more important. There are so many strategic possibilities to consider, particularly if you are playing a well-designed golf course. This section attempts to cover most of the situations you are likely to encounter that require sound strategy before executing the shot. Many of the tips also show you how to tailor your strategy to the particular strengths and weaknesses of your own game.

Section 10:

CONTENTS

MASTER·STROKES

The "Center Of Green" Experiment

If you are a middle-to-high handicap golfer looking for a way to cut your score, try this experiment in course strategy next time you play: On all full-approach shots, just try to hit the center of the green. Don't worry about where the flag is located. Simply play a safe shot toward the green's center and accept the putt you have remaining. If you hit the middle of just about any green, you won't be too far from the hole, and you'll have greatly reduced the odds of finding any severe trouble guarding the green. Play 18 holes using this approach, and you might be very surprised at the score you shoot!

MASTER·STROKES

Accept A Bogey

Many golfers hurt their scores by trying "miracle" shots that are outside their capabilities, in order to save a par. When you get in a trouble situation off the tee, for example in deep rough with the next shot needing to carry a hazard, keep in mind that making a bogey will not ruin your score. If you know you can't slash the ball all the way to the green on the fly, don't bother trying for a miracle. Lay up short of the hazards and try to get on the green in one stroke above regulation.

If you make no more than a bogey every time you are in trouble, when you've finished you'll be pleasantly surprised with your score.

MASTER·STROKES

Level Stance, Easier Shot

Maintaining balance is an underrated factor in hitting solid shots, and it's more challenging to keep your balance as you get older. If you play a hilly course, whenever possible, aim your shots to finish on a level lie rather than a steep one. You particularly want to avoid downhill lies which make it hard to get the next shot airborne. So on a hole where a long drive will put your next shot on a downhill lie, you're better off hitting a 3-wood or 5-wood off the tee to keep the ball short of the downslope. While you'll have a slightly longer second shot, it will be one you're much more likely to swing at confidently and hit successfully.

MASTER·STROKES

"Overclub" To Get Pin-High

About 80 percent of all amateurs underclub their approach shots. Here's a great tip to help you get more shots pin-high. Assume the pin is at middle depth on the green and that any trouble is not much greater in front of the green than over it, or vice versa. Select the club that, if you hit it perfectly, would reach the back fringe of the green. That's right, let your "perfect" hits be a little long! The reason for this is you will hit the majority of your shots a little less than perfectly; let all these "average" shots finish pin-high! The extra benefit of this club selection approach is that your most poorly-struck shots, instead of finishing way short, may end up reaching the front of the green.

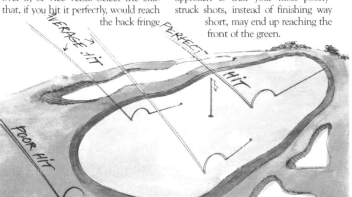

MASTER·STROKES

Plan the Par-Fives

Even if you don't hit the ball as far as you would like to, with a good game plan, the par-fives are still your best bet for birdies. However, whaling away in hopes of reaching the green in two on a 500-yard hole rarely works. Instead, your aim should be to hit a safe tee shot with a club you are confident you can hit the fairway with. If you can put the ball in the fairway just 200 yards out, you have in effect turned this par-5 hole into a 300-yard par-4. From here, you can try for another safe shot that leaves you and open short iron or wedge to the flag. You can make as many birdies on the par-fives with finesse as with power.

200 YDS.

200 YDS.

100 YDS.

MASTER·STROKES

Avoid A Watery Grave

Every so often you'll face a substantial carry over a water hazard. You can make the distance, but it's a tough shot.

Be realistic. Consider the distance and the lie before you choose your club. You might think you can get home with a 4-iron; however, you'd have to hit it perfectly to carry the ball to the green. If there's no major trouble over the green, you're much better off choosing a longer club than you think you need, in this case a 5-wood. If you hit it perfectly and end up slightly long, you shouldn't have a difficult recovery.

Knowing you've taken "plenty of club" allows you to make a relaxed swing, reducing the chance of a mis-hit that puts the ball in a "watery grave."

MASTER STROKES

AIM FOR FADE

Play "Your" Shot

Every golfer likes to hit the ball long, high and straight, but experience tells you that you can expect a certain pattern to your shots. It may be a low hook or a high fade. Keep in mind that even if your particular shot isn't pretty, it can still be functional as long as it's predictable. On the course during a match, don't try to fight your shot. If your drives tend to slice 15 to 20 yards, plan for that as you aim. If your middle iron approaches fade 5 to 10 yards, take that into account too. Work on improving your ball flight on the practice tee, but play with what you've got on the course.

MASTER STROKES

The "Sure Thing" Layup

Often during a round you will need to hit a shot that stays short of a hazard. When hitting a layup shot, many golfers make the mistake of choosing too long of a club—a club with which they may reach the hazard if they hit it perfectly.

If you decide to lay up, make it a "sure thing." Select a club with which you are certain you cannot reach the hazard, even if you catch the shot perfectly and it also takes an extra-large bounce. For example, if the hazard is 190 yards away, select a club you will ordinarily hit no more than 160 yards. This way, if the ball "flies" and/or you get a big bounce, you'll still be safely short.

160

190

MASTER·STROKES

Leave Pin In On Downhill Chips

On shots from just off the green, you may leave the pin in or have it removed. Some golfers like to take the pin out when they have a chance to sink it, thinking that the pin may stop the ball from going in. If the chip shot is downhill, or if the green is simply fast, leave the pin in. On a downhill chip, there's a greater chance you'll hit the delicate shot too hard. If this is the case and you hit the shot on line, the pin will at least stop the ball from going as far as it would have had the pin been removed, and, if the ball hits it dead square, it may still drop in. Either way, you're better off with the pin in.

MASTER·STROKES

Carry Shots In Wet Conditions

Golfers who usually don't hit the ball a long way have a tougher time when the course is wet because low shots that normally give them good roll are instead stopping quickly. In wet weather, hit all your shots to carry as far as possible in the air. Adjust the clubs in your set accordingly. This may mean leaving your driver out of the bag if you tend to hit it low, and teeing off with a 3-wood. Also, if your longest iron is, say, a 4-iron, consider taking it out of the bag and using a 7-wood or 9-wood instead. Finally, aim all your approach shots to land nearly all the way to the flag. You'll get the most out of your score this way when it's wet.

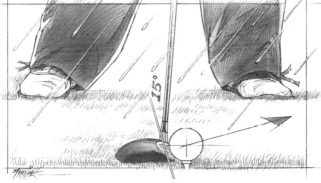

MASTER·STROKES

Use Longer Club in Cold Weather

Golf shots play much differently when it's 40 degrees as opposed to 80 degrees. In cold conditions, you won't be able to carry the ball as far or hit it as high as in the summertime. Don't fight this reality, but rather, allow for it. If the shot calls for a 5-iron in warm conditions, drop down to a 4-iron. Plan for a shot that will fly lower and land a little short of the green and then run up onto it. Refrain from trying to overpower shots in cold conditions, and you can shoot some surprisingly good scores, even in chilly weather.

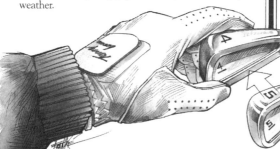

°F
120
100
80
60
40
20
0

MASTER STROKES

Tee Up On Trouble Side

You'll sometimes encounter holes that have severe trouble (water, woods, out-of-bounds) on one side. Meanwhile, no dangerous hazards lurk on the opposite side. When it is imperative to that you steer clear of hazards down one side, always tee up your ball on the same side of the tee as the trouble lies. This makes it much easier to angle your setup and clubface alignment so that you are aiming away from the severe trouble. This simple strategic tip will usually help you steer clear of hitting your drive into major trouble and thus avoid making a "big number."

MASTER·STROKES

Read Rough Before Selecting Club

Pitching Wedge

7 Wood

5 Iron

You'll get the most out of recovery shots if you know how your lie in the rough will affect the shot, and then select the club that the lie will allow you to hit. The deeper the rough, the more loft you'll need. However, pay attention to the direction the grass is growing. Say the grass is three inches long and is growing away from the target. It will resist the club's movement much more than normal. You might need a 9-iron or pitching wedge to get the ball up and out. However, if the same-length rough is growing toward the target, it will offer much less resistance. You may find you can use a 5-iron or a 7-wood effectively. Knowing this will help you escape the rough as well as many stronger players.

MASTER·STROKES

"Measure" The Dogleg

Often, longer holes have fairways that bend or "dogleg." Usually the dogleg is in the landing area for the tee shot. It's a great temptation to try to "cut the corner" and lessen the distance of the second shot. Keep in mind that doglegs also present problems: If you try to cut the corner on a dogleg that's beyond your driving distance, you'll be blocked out on your approach shot. So before you decide to cut the corner, be sure of the distance such a shot requires. If you can't carry your drive past the corner, aim for the side of the fairway away from the dogleg. Although your next shot will be longer, you'll have a clear opening to the green.

MASTER·STROKES

Ignore the Big Hitter

Many golfers are intimidated by physically strong players who can drive the ball substantially farther. Remember that success in golf is not about who hits the longest drive, but who takes the fewest strokes. A player who concentrates on square contact and keeps the ball in play, and who has an effective short game, can easily outscore a player who is erratic.

Next time you play against a long knocker, commit to your own game, with an emphasis on a controlled swing off the tee, and rely on your wedge and putter to save some pars. You may find that with this approach, you can unsettle — and outscore — a much longer hitter.

MASTER·STROKES

Set Your Personal Par

Many golfers frustrate themselves and play worse than they should, because they expect too much in terms of score. Midway through the round, when it's obvious they can't reach their lofty goal, their games fall completely apart.

Maybe you're not quite the player you once were. Instead of 80 being a realistic goal, 83 is more reasonable on an average day. Suppose also that today it's raining a bit and windy, so the course is playing extra long and tough. It's better to realize that under these conditions, an 86 would be a good score for you. Be realistic about your game and the current conditions, and you'll take a lot of pressure off so you enjoy the game more and score better.

MASTER·STROKES

7iron

Play For Position

Nearly all amateurs will shoot lower scores if their goal on tee shots on the longer holes is to hit the ball to a specific target, rather than for sheer distance. You'll never drive the ball accurately if you're trying to hit it as hard as you can, yet that's what so many high handicappers do. Instead, pick a spot on the fairway that is 1) easily within reach, 2) gives you a good angle to shoot to the green or your next target down the fairway, and 3) leaves you with a level stance and lie. Once you've determined this target, take your driver (or a shorter club) and play your tee shot as if you were hitting a smooth 7-iron to a green. You'll be surprised at how little distance you lose and how much accuracy you gain.

MASTER STROKES

Par 4 367 yds.

When To Forget the Driver

You've played several holes, have used your driver three times and have missed the fairway badly each time—twice left and once right. So far you have avoided any disasters, but your course has a number of holes coming up that demand accuracy. You wonder if you can start driving the ball straight.

When this is the case, do what most amateurs don't—put the driver away for the rest of the day! Use your 3-wood or any lofted wood you have more confidence in. Going to a more lofted club will make it much easier to keep the ball in play, since the more lofted club puts more backspin on the ball. The accuracy you gain will far outweigh the slight distance loss. Work on your driver technique on the practice after the round, rather than paying the price during it.

MASTER·STROKES

When To Rip It

While most amateurs overswing even when distance is not crucial, there are times when you can and should go for extra distance off the tee. Look for holes where two factors exist: 1. There is plenty of fairway and no severe trouble should you stray a little; 2. Getting extra distance off the tee could allow you to get home in two rather than three (on a long par-4 or short par-5).

If you decide it's time to "rip it," a good tip is to start the driver back slower and lower to the ground than usual. This will help you obtain maximum width in your swing arc, and allow you to build your speed gradually to unleash at impact.

MASTER·STROKES

When "Short" Is Okay

Sometimes you'll play a course with greens that are open in front. However, their sides are well-guarded, the greens slope steeply from back to front, and hitting over the green sends the ball into trouble down an embankment. Being long (or off line) on your approach shots can cost you a stroke, sometimes two.

While most amateurs tend to underclub on approach shots, in this situation it's a good idea to try to keep your shot short of the hole. This way, if you hit the green you'll have an uphill rather than a fast downhill putt. And if your shot comes up short, you'll still have a fairly simple uphill chip.

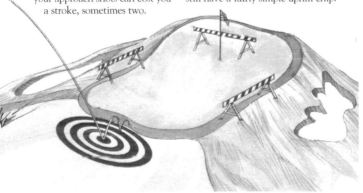

MASTER·STROKES

Smart Seconds Into Par-5s

When you can't reach a par-5 in two (which is most of the time), you should play a second shot which leaves the easiest possible approach to the green. This may not simply mean hitting your 3-wood as far as you can. Analyze each second shot on par-5s — every situation will be different. Often, hitting a good 3-wood will leave you, say,

TEE SHOT

100 YDS. OUT

60 YDS. OUT

BETTER APPROACH

50-75 yards to the green — a less-than-full wedge shot that may be tougher to get close than a full wedge. Also, say the pin is tucked to the left side. You'd have a much easier third if you could place your second shot on the right edge of the fairway. So consider both the distance you want to leave to the green and the desirable angle to the flag, then select club and shot accordingly.

MASTER·STROKES

Use Opening On Approach Shots

On the majority of holes you play, the front of the green will be relatively open while any hazards lie to the sides or rear of the green. When you have an open line to the flag, keep in mind that you don't have to fly the ball all the way to the green. Particularly on shots with less-lofted clubs, and especially if the ground is fairly firm, plan for a shot that lands in the opening five to 10 yards short of the green, then rolls up. By using the openings that are available, you take pressure off your swing to "carry" the ball all the way; chances are good you'll hit a more solid and accurate shot.

MASTER·STROKES

Match Play Strategies

You'll be most successful in match play by simply concentrating on making the lowest possible score on every hole, regardless of what your opponent is doing. There are some exceptions to this rule, however. Say you're playing a medium-short par-4. Your opponent, hitting first, drives out of bounds left. With his next ball, he'll be hitting three off the tee, so in effect you have a two-stroke advantage. Here you'd be wise to aim on a safer line than usual, well right. Also, since it's a hole that's easily reachable in two, you might tee off with a fairway wood instead of a driver for greater accuracy. In these instances conservative execution is all you're likely to need to win the hole.

Driver

Fairway Wood

MASTER·STROKES

Altitude Affects Distance

During summer months, many golfers vacation in different regions of the country. Keep in mind if you travel that the golf ball does not fly the same distance everywhere. If you normally play at sea level and are vacationing high in the mountains, the ball will fly about 10 per- cent farther than normal. This means if you normally hit a 5-iron 160 yards, it will travel about 176 yards at high altitude. So adjust your club selection accordingly. Just the opposite is also true: If you live at a high altitude and are vacationing near the ocean, the ball will not fly as far. Take at least one, and perhaps two, clubs stronger on your approach shots.

longer club   *shorter club*

MASTER·STROKES

Learn From Opponent's Putt

Often you can gain valuable information from the shot your opponent or another member of your foursome is about to play. Say your ball is 15 feet from the hole. Another player has a 25-foot putt along a similar line. Pay careful attention to the roll of his or her ball from the moment it reaches the area where you will putt from until it reaches the hole. You may see that the ball broke a little more or less than you thought it would. Or perhaps it's pulled up short, indicating that the green might be a little slower than you imagined. Be alert to the information available before you step up to your own putt, and you'll make more of them.

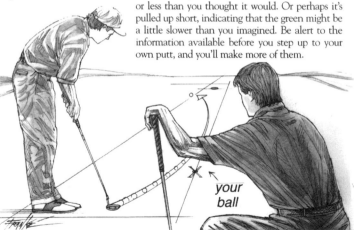

your ball

MASTER·STROKES

Use Tee Slopes To Your Advantage

Did you ever notice that on a well-built golf course, the teeing areas are not quite flat? Most teeing areas are slightly crowned. That is, the highest point is in the center, so water will drain to the sides. You can use this fact to your advantage. If you tee up on the left side of the tee, the ball will be a trifle above your feet. This helps if you want to hit a shot that draws from right to left. If you tee up on the right side of a tee that is crowned, conversely, the ball will be slightly below your feet. The tendency from this position is to fade the ball from left to right. So if the hole calls for a fade and the tee is crowned, tee up on the right side to take advantage.

MASTER·STROKES

Use Depth Of Tee on Par-3s

The teeing area is actually a rectangle. This rectangle is the area within a line between the two tee markers, to a depth behind the markers equal to two club lengths. Thus the teeing area is about two and a half yards deep (the length of two drivers). It helps to know this, especially on par-threes. Say you're unsure whether to hit a hard 7-iron or a smooth 6- from the tee. If you choose the 7-iron, tee up on the forward line between the markers. If you opt for the smooth 6-, drop back to the rear of the imaginary rectangle. Either way, if you judge and strike the shot as planned, your shot will finish a little closer to the perfect distance.

7 iron

6 iron

MASTER·STROKES

Work Back From Flag To Tee

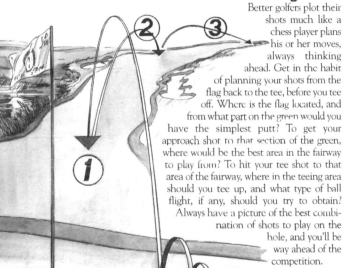

Better golfers plot their shots much like a chess player plans his or her moves, always thinking ahead. Get in the habit of planning your shots from the flag back to the tee, before you tee off. Where is the flag located, and from what part on the green would you have the simplest putt? To get your approach shot to that section of the green, where would be the best area in the fairway to play from? To hit your tee shot to that area of the fairway, where in the teeing area should you tee up, and what type of ball flight, if any, should you try to obtain? Always have a picture of the best combination of shots to play on the hole, and you'll be way ahead of the competition.

UPHILL PUTT →

FRANK

MASTER·STROKES

Set Up Your Layups

The smart golfer will lay up short of hazards rather than trying for a long carry that requires a perfect hit. You'll help your score even more by "setting up" you layup to give you the easiest possible shot to the pin.

Say you're laying up short of an elevated green guarded by a deep bunker. The green sits on a diagonal to the fairway with the pin at the right rear — a difficult spot. Do the following: 1) Aim for the left side of the fairway — this leaves a diagonal shot angle, giving you more green to hit short of the flag: 2) Lay up well short so your next shot is 70-85 yards rather than 40-50. This way you can hit a fuller shot with your sand wedge to put maximum backspin on the ball.

EASIER SHOT TO HOLE.

MASTER·STROKES

Use the Right Opening

You've sliced your drive into trees, 175 yards left to the green. Looking over your shot, you see a line between the trees to the green, but you would need to thread the ball through a six-foot-wide opening 25 yards ahead. You also have a wide opening to pitch the ball diagonally back to the fairway. This would leave a shot of about 100 yards for your third. What do you do?

In a case like this, the amateur should almost always play the safe recovery. The odds of hitting a tree when going for the green are just too great. Simply play through the safe opening back to the middle of the fairway. Take your chances from there on hitting a good pitch that leaves you with a makeable putt for a par.

MASTER·STROKES

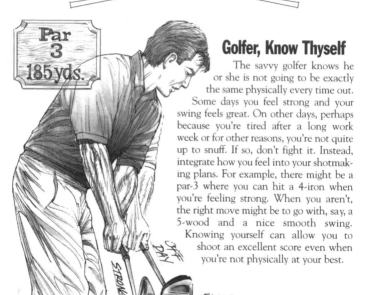

Par 3
185 yds.

STRONG DAY
OFF DAY
– 4 IRON
– 5 WOOD

Golfer, Know Thyself

The savvy golfer knows he or she is not going to be exactly the same physically every time out. Some days you feel strong and your swing feels great. On other days, perhaps because you're tired after a long work week or for other reasons, you're not quite up to snuff. If so, don't fight it. Instead, integrate how you feel into your shotmaking plans. For example, there might be a par-3 where you can hit a 4-iron when you're feeling strong. When you aren't, the right move might be to go with, say, a 5-wood and a nice smooth swing. Knowing yourself can allow you to shoot an excellent score even when you're not physically at your best.

MASTER·STROKES

Adjust For Uphill / Downhill Targets

When approaching a green that's either well above or below, most amateurs don't take the elevation change into consideration when choosing a club.

When the target is steeply uphill, the upslope will cut off the downward flight of the ball earlier than normal. To a green well below, the ball's downward flight will continue farther.

Keep in mind that the longer the shot, the more you'll need to adjust, because the lower trajectory of the longer club will be affected more. For example, if for a level shot a 3-iron would be needed, you might need to make a two-club adjustment; but on a 9-iron shot which descends more steeply, you'll likely need one club more or less.

MASTER·STROKES

How Conditions Alter Club Selection

You may know that you hit your 6-iron an average of, say 150 yards. Does this mean every time you're 150 yards out, you should use a 6-iron? No! Weather and ground conditions for any situation must be factored in, and in extreme cases this can cause a huge difference in club selection. If it's cold, the wind is against you, the shot is uphill, and the ground where the ball will land is soft, you may need a 3-iron or even a 5-wood to cover the 150 yards. On the other hand, if it's hot, the shot is downhill and downwind, the ground is hard, and your ball is sitting in light rough that will make it "fly" with little backspin, the correct club may be a 9-iron or even a pitching wedge. Consider all factors before choosing a club.

MASTER·STROKES

Focus On Fairways Hit

Most golfers are concerned with how far they hit their drives. Did you ever consider how many drives you hit in the fairway?

On most courses there are 14 longer holes (with four par-3's). In your last few rounds, how many tee shots finished in the fairway? If you average nine fairways or less, you've identified an area of your game that needs work. If you average six or fewer fairways hit, you must improve your driving accuracy. You'll hit many more greens in regulation if you hit more approaches from the fairway, and you'll have fewer really bad holes. So focus on hitting more fairways. Swing your driver with more control or tee off with a shorter club if necessary. Your scores will immediately improve.

MASTER STROKES

Don't Keep Score!

Most amateurs spend too much time worrying about how they're scoring at any given point in the round. If they're playing well, they try to "protect" their score. Or if they're doing poorly, they press for birdies in their desperation to "catch up." Either way, they can only hurt their performance in the remainder of the round. Try this experiment over the next several rounds. Don't keep score at all during play. Focus your complete attention on what each shot requires; don't worry about the results. After you're finished, take a scorecard, review your round, and fill the card out. You'll probably be surprised at how well you scored!

PRODUCTIVE PRACTICE

Many readers, no doubt, will be tempted to skip this section. That's because they never practice! It is the sincere hope here that you at least read through this extensive section. There are so many ways that the practice techniques described here can help your game. As you read them, you'll see that "practice" means much more than just dumping a big bucket of balls on the practice range and then slogging away. Granted, that can be boring; but what you'll see here are a number of ways to practice which can actually be lots of fun. You will learn to play "games" in practice, whether it's against yourself or with a partner. You will learn how to practice for specific shots and situations, and you'll build confidence for the times when these situations arise on the course.

Pick out one or two of the practice tips that follow and give them a try. Later, you might come back for more.

CONTENTS

MASTER STROKES

Vary Your Practice Sequence

When most golfers practice, they start with their shortest wedge and work their way through the bag, finishing with the driver. While it's wise to start with small wedges, it's also a good idea to vary the order in which you hit all the clubs. Otherwise, you'll tend to swing harder and harder as the clubs lengthen, so that by the end you're overswinging with the driver.

Try this instead: Once you've loosened up by hitting the wedges, hit some 3-woods, then some 7-irons, then some drivers, then finish up, say, with the 5-iron. This varied sequence will teach you to use the same tempo and swing force with all the clubs in your bag, and will breed more consistent shotmaking on the course.

WEDGE

3 WOOD

7 IRON

DRIVER

5 IRON

Franke

MASTER·STROKES

Keep A Level Head

Many amateurs allow their heads to bob up and down during the swing. This results in topped or fat shots, depending on the head's position at impact.

Here's a drill to check whether your head is staying level: At address, have a friend stand behind you, holding a club parallel to the ground so that the grip end rests lightly atop your head. Hit a shot while your friend holds the club steady. If you lose contact with the club, you know your head bobbed down, and your friend can tell you if your head pushes the club up. Hit practice shots with the club acting as a "governor" to help you get the feel of a level head. Consistently solid shots on the course will result.

MASTER STROKES

Putting Matches To Keep You Sharp

You should practice your putting frequently, however, golfers don't do enough of it. To sharpen your touch while having fun, try the following putting match with a playing partner: Select a putt on the putting green. Try to sink the putt while concentrating on rolling the ball at the correct speed. If your putt finishes short of the hole, you score zero points. If the ball goes more than two feet past the hole, you also score zero. If the ball reaches the hole yet finishes no more than two feet past, you score one point. If you hole the putt, score three points. Play a 9- or 18-hole match. The player with the highest point total wins. Play this game frequently and your touch will improve quickly!

3 pts.

Zero pts.

1 point

Zero pts.

MASTER STROKES

"Fairways & Greens" Practice

To make your practice-range sessions more productive, try "fairways & greens" practice, as if playing your home course shot by shot.

Take out the club you would hit from the first tee. Tee up and pick out two markers such as yardage signs or trees, to serve as boundaries of the "fairway." Hit your drive and determine whether it hit the fairway. Next, take out the club you'd need to hit the first green. Aim for a specific target, and determine whether your shot finished "on the green."

Hit all full shots your course requires. When you finish, write down how many fairways and greens you hit during your "round," and strive to better your average each time you practice.

MASTER·STROKES

Lift Back Foot At Finish

Shorter hitters need to concentrate on actively shifting their body weight through the shot for maximum club-head speed and power. However, they instead leave too much weight on the back foot through and past impact.

Here's a drill to try on the practice tee, using an iron: Hit the shot with a controlled swing, and as you move into the follow-through, lift your right foot off the ground. If this is difficult to do, it means you had too much weight on your right side and were not shifting your weight actively enough. Keep working on lifting your right foot and balancing on your left on the fol-low-through, and you'll ingrain the feel of a strong weight shift through the ball.

MASTER STROKES

Practice Wedge Distances

70 YDS.
60 YDS.
50 YDS.
40 YDS.

If you aren't hitting as many greens in regulation as you once did, your short game must be sharper. And, controlling the distance of short pitch shots is a key to saving pars. Remember that it's much easier to hit a less-than-full shot on line than it is to hit it the perfect distance.

To sharpen your short wedge game, on the practice tee, set out targets such as towels or ball buckets at 10-yard increments, from 40 to 70 yards out. Try to hit pitch shots the precise distance to these targets. Vary your target with each shot, trying to hit one shot 50 yards, the next 40, the next 70, and so on. Such practice will pay off on the course.

MASTER·STROKES

Putt To A Tee

Here's a simple tip that may help you hole an extra putt or two: On the practice putting green before teeing off, don't putt toward the cup. Instead, stick a golf tee in the ground, then practice putting toward it from various distances and angles. Figure that you've "made" the putt only when your ball makes contact with the tee while it's rolling fairly slowly.

Putting to a tee in effect shrinks the size of your target, which heightens your concentration. When you get out onto the first green, the hole will look large and inviting.

MASTER STROKES

"1-2-3 Hit"

Many capable amateurs hit shots far below their potential because they tighten up over the ball and make a quick, tense swing. Here's a practice-tee drill that will teach you to freewheel through the ball as you should:

1. Start at address with your club two feet from the ball and make your normal, full practice swing. **2.** Step forward so the clubhead is one foot away from the ball and without hesitation, make a second full practice swing. **3.** Step forward, place the clubhead behind the ball, and immediately take your third "practice" swing – this time, actually hitting the ball!

Use this "1-2-3 Hit" drill and soon your on-course swing will be much freer.

HIT ← **3** ← **2** ← **1**

MASTER STROKES

Make "Little" Driver Swings

There's little doubt that most amateurs swing too hard with the driver. Here's a drill to use as you finish your warmup: Tee up a ball and make a very small driver swing, as if you're hitting a long chip. Try to hit the ball only 100 yards. With the next swing, try to hit it just 125 yards, then 150. Gradually increase your swing length, but as you finish up, you should still feel like your swing is well below maximum effort. When you go to the first tee, keep the image of these "soft" driver swings in mind. You'll be surprised at how well you drive the ball.

150 yds.

MASTER·STROKES

Games Good Chippers Play

To score your best, you must get the ball "up and down" with a good chip and one putt when your approach finishes a little off the putting surface. You should practice greenside chip shots often. Here's a way to make it fun and productive.

Drop three balls by the edge of the practice green. Chip them toward one hole, then move to another spot and choose another target. Your goal is to chip one ball into the cup: You can't leave until you hole at least one! When this gets too easy, set a goal to hole two chips, then three. The trick is always to stay until you've met your goal. You'll sharpen your feel and soon get most of your chips to finish very close.

MASTER·STROKES

Practice With Teed-Up Ball

Many seniors gradually develop pain in various joints when making the swing, particularly in the hands, wrists, elbows and shoulders. It may get to the point where you are playing less and never practicing, so your game gets worse. Here's an idea that will help: On the practice range, hit shots off a tee with all your clubs, rather than hitting them off the ground. You only need to tee the ball up a quarter of an inch. Striking the ball off a tee rather than hitting off the ground removes the stress that moves through your hands and arms every time your clubhead smashes into the turf. You'll have less pain and injury in the long run.

MASTER·STROKES

Swing From "Toe Up" to "Toe Up"

It's far easier to deliver a square clubface at impact if you keep it square in relation to the path of the swing for as long as possible. Here's a good practice tip: Take your longest iron (which has a relatively flat clubface) and practice making half swings with the clubshaft moving back and through only parallel to the ground in either direction. When the shaft is parallel either on the backswing or the follow-through, the toe of the club should be pointing straight up, rather than angled in front of you or behind you. Practice this correct "toe up" position on either side of the ball until it becomes second nature. You'll find yourself delivering the clubface naturally and squarely through impact.

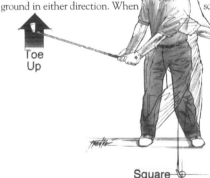

Toe Up

Toe Up

Square

MASTER·STROKES

"Billiard" Putting

Better golfers know their success rate on short putts — three to six feet — can make the difference between a fine round and a mediocre one. Here's a game to make practicing short putts more fun: Place three balls around the front lip of the cup, 4-6 inches away. Then pick out which ball you want to knock in with the ball you putt — sort of like playing a billiard shot. To angle any of the stationary balls into the cup, you must putt much more precisely than you would to simply hole the ball you putt.

"Billiard" putting practice is not only fun, but will increase your concentration and demand more precision. A half-hour of this practice will make the hole look like a barrel out on the course!

MASTER STROKES

The Split-Hand Drill

Here's a drill that teaches the correct rotation of your forearms during the swing, in which your right forearm crosses freely over your left through the impact zone. Standing upright, take a middle iron and grip it normally, holding the clubshaft horizontally in front of you. Then slide your right hand to the bottom of the

grip, so there's a space of three to four inches between your hands. Next, swing the clubhead back and forth in front of you. Notice how the right forearm crosses over the left as you swing through.

Try this drill for a couple of minutes on the practice tee, then go ahead and hit some balls. You'll feel a freer arm swing and see shots that fly higher and farther.

MASTER·STROKES

The Right-Foot-Up Drill

A great many amateurs make poor contact and lack power because they fail to shift their weight fully onto their left or front foot on the downswing. Here's a drill to help you get the feel of getting your weight where it belongs: Take an object such as a sturdy box that is 8-10 inches tall. (You can also use an upside-down range ball basket.) Set up to an iron shot with your right foot atop the box or basket, but with nearly all your weight on your left foot. Go ahead and hit shots from this position. The drill will ingrain the feel of having your weight on your left side at impact as you should, and this feeling will feed into your regular swing out on the course.

weight left

MASTER·STROKES

Practice From the Sand

Most greenside sand shots are not that difficult, but they all vary somewhat. They require a "feel" for both the situation and the slight mechanical adjustments that come with each shot.

Most amateurs rarely practice bunker shots. Therefore they may see a certain bunker situation only rarely, and when they do they don't know how to handle it. If your course has a practice bunker, use it! Hit 50 bunker shots every week, from various distances, lies and stances. If your course does not have a practice bunker, go out to one on the course in the evening when it's quiet, and practice for 10 or 15 minutes. You'll soon feel much more comfortable on these shots.

DOWNHILL

NORMAL LIE

UPHILL

MASTER·STROKES

WORST

BEST

"Worst Ball" Practice

If you want to toughen your game, try this practice technique when the course isn't busy: Play two balls off the tee. Then select your worst of the two tee shots. Say it's in the left rough. From there, play two balls, and select your worst recovery shot.

Play two shots to the green from there, and so on until you've holed out.

At first you'll be discouraged, because your "worst ball" score will be really high! Remember it's just practice. It teaches you to make controlled swings all the way around the course, and think out the right shots to play from trouble. The result will be much more controlled play and lower scores in your regular rounds.

MASTER·STROKES

Practice From Uneven Lies

Amateurs often wonder, "Why do I hit the ball so much better on the practice range?" They forget that on the practice tee, they're hitting shots only from level stances. On rolling to hilly courses, you'll face many fairway shots where the ball is above or below your feet, or the lie is uphill or downhill.

Practice from uneven lies every chance you can. Often the sides of the practice tee will be sloping, so that you can find spots to practice iron shots with the ball above or below your feet, or from uphill or downhill lies. Remember to stay steady over the ball and swing within yourself. Soon you'll be handling these shots more expertly on the course.

MASTER·STROKES

Concentrate On The Short Game

Every golfer would like to hit each green in regulation and shoot for birdies every time, but even the pros can't accomplish this. The higher your handicap and the more problems you have with your long game, the more essential it is to have a tidy short game. Without it, pars will be hard to come by.

Make a decision that this season, you will spend the majority of your practice time on your short game pitches from 50 yards in, chipping, sand shots, and putting as opposed to just practicing full shots. Stick with this commitment for the entire season and you will do your best scoring in years.

MASTER·STROKES

Feet-Together Practice

Good balance is the most overlooked aspect of a consistent swing. If you're off-balance through impact, you won't make square, solid contact.

The best way to improve balance is to practice hitting shots with your feet together. Take your driver. Stand with the insides of your feet nearly touching and make a swing. If you swing too hard and try to shift too much weight either going back or through, you'll fall over! Now take out an 8- or 9-iron and hit shots with your feet together. Make very smooth, three-quarter swings. Notice how much better your balance is. On the course, with your normal stance, maintain the same swing action. You'll hit much more consistent shots.

MASTER STROKES

Putt A Range Ball

If you're not making many putts, chances are you're not stroking the ball squarely. The ball is not rolling with a pure end-over-end motion but is wobbling instead. This type of putt will often "lip out," while the putt that is rolling end-over-end seems to "try" to drop in.

Try this. Go to the practice green with a range ball that has a stripe around it. Select as straight a putt as possible. Line up the ball's stripe exactly toward the hole, then hit your putt. Did the stripe wobble, or did it roll perfectly end-over-end? Keep practicing with the goal to make the ball's stripe roll perfectly straight, and you'll start to see your putts drop out on the course.

MASTER·STROKES

"Bank" Your Practice

You may have heard a golfing friend say, "Gee, I practiced a lot the last few days and I still shot a bad score. Why bother practicing?"

Keep in mind that as long as you are practicing sound fundamentals, in the long run, the more you practice the better you will play. Remember that there will usually be a time lag between the work you put in and when this work pays off. Practicing today doesn't guarantee a great round tomorrow. Think of a practice session as a small contribution into your golfing "bank account." The more practice sessions you can work into your schedule over the course of a season, the more you'll see your handicap go down.

MASTER·STROKES

Add "Snap" To Your Downswing

Here's a practice drill for golfers looking to increase distance on their shots: Take an old driver and hold it upside down. Grip it in your right hand only, just above the club-head. Position the club as you would at the top of the backswing. Now, as you swing down and through, try to make as loud a "whoosh" at impact as you can. To do so, you'll need to actively snap your right hand and forearm through the impact zone. Also, you'll generate maximum speed when you push off with your right foot and the inside of your right leg. Learn to use your right arm and leg to create that extra "whoosh," and you'll see longer shots on the course.

WHOOSH

MASTER·STROKES

WITH WIND

INTO WIND
YES

Practice
Into the Wind

You'll gain much more information about your swing and your shotmaking if you practice into the wind whenever you can. Why? Into the wind, any errors in your ball-striking will be magnified. For example, a shot that might fade 10 yards to the right with no wind, will slice about 20 yards into a firm breeze. If you hit the same shot downwind, the breeze would decrease the amount of spin so the ball would fly nearly straight (and farther), giving you false information.

Practicing into the wind will train you to deliver the club as squarely as possible to the ball. Final tip: Never try to hit the ball hard into the wind. Swing smoothly and you'll find the ball bores through the wind better.

MASTER·STROKES

"Tough Club" Practice

There's a trend, and it's wise for seniors, toward using more of the highly-lofted fairway woods because they're easier to hit. This is fine. Keep in mind though that easy-to-hit clubs can, over time, make your swing sloppier since you can "get away" with slightly poorer contact.

If you're hoping to improve ball-striking quality, try "tough club" practice. Take an old club that was difficult to hit consistently well (a 1-, 2-, or 3-iron). Go to the practice range and work with this club. Concentrate on making the best possible contact. While you'll hit some shots that don't look good, this practice will make your swing more precise so that on the course, you'll see the benefits.

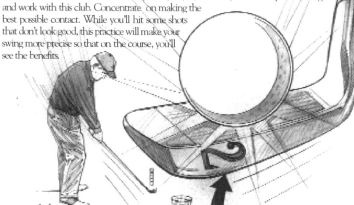

MASTER·STROKES

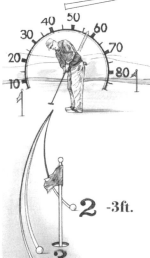

2 -3ft.

3

1 +4ft.

Sharpen Your Long-Putt Touch

On putts of 40 feet and longer, correct distance is harder to obtain than accurate line. Here's a drill to help. Pick out a long downhill putt on the practice green.

Take three balls. Try to deliberately roll the first putt four feet past. Then try to stop the second putt three feet short. Now that you know the feel for being a little short or long, try to roll the third one at the perfect speed, so that it stops just a bit beyond the hole. Now do the same drill with a long uphill putt, and with other putts that have varying speeds. You'll find your feel for speed on long putts improving quickly on the course.

MASTER·STROKES

Practice Lofted Woods From Rough

Many seniors have added lofted fairway woods (5, 7, and 9) to their sets in place of long irons. While this is wise, remember that lofted woods have clubfaces that are often shallow from top to bottom. This makes them easier to hit from the fairway, from hard ground, or when the ball is down in the rough. But sometimes you'll get lies in rough where the ball is perched up (lower drawing). These can be tricky: The shallow clubface can slide under the ball, popping it straight up.

Practice shots from the rough with your lofted woods from these "up" lies, using a sweeping rather than digging motion, and these clubs will become your ally in any situation.

MASTER·STROKES

Pass The Ball

If you lack distance, you need to remember that the swing will be most powerful and efficient when you use the entire body, rather than just the arms, to swing the club. Here's a drill to aid your backswing turn: Stand as you would at address, except that you are not holding a club. Without moving your feet, turn to your right, as if you were handing a ball to another person. Make sure that in handing off the ball, you turn your upper body fully, so your sternum is facing the person taking the hand-off. Practice this move often, then incorporate it into your swing on the practice range, and finally on the course. You'll soon see solid shots with a longer and higher flight.

MASTER·STROKES

Short Game "Games"

You can never put in too much work on your short game. Following is a way to make practice more fun, whether by yourself or competing against a friend.

Basic Chip: Play 10 chip shots from just off the green, 35-50 feet from hole. Score 5 points for a hole-out, 2 points for shots within two feet, 1 point for shots within four feet. Short Pitch-and-Run: Play 10 shots from 10-15 yards off the green, 60-90 feet from hole. Score 10 points for a hole-out, 2 points within 4 feet, 1 point within 8 feet. Greenside Bunker Shot: Play 10 shots from normal lie, 40-60 feet from hole. Score 20 points for a hole-out, 2 points within 6 feet, 1 point within 12 feet. Count your total points, and always try to top it the next time.

MASTER·STROKES

Practice With Smaller Driver

If you've played golf for a number of years, you've seen how the size of clubheads have changed, particularly the driver. Today's driver heads are much larger and more forgiving than the early metalwoods of some 20 years ago. Yet, if you have an older, smaller-headed driver (of either wood or metal), it can serve a useful purpose as a practice tool. Try practicing with a smaller-headed driver. Because this driver is less forgiving, it will encourage you to focus on swinging the club under control and on making the squarest possible contact. This will add consistency to your tee shots, no matter how big your current club is!

GAME
DAY
DRIVER →

PRACTICE
DRIVER→

MASTER·STROKES

"Creative" Practice

There is no one "standard" swing that will serve every situation on the course. Good golfers can "create" swings to meet unusual circumstances: shots that must be hooked or sliced around trees, kept low to stay below branches, hit high to carry trees or mounds, hit with extra backspin to stop quickly, or even hit left-handed (for a righty)! Don't wait until you are in trouble to play the shot for the first time. On the practice tee, imagine situations where you must play a low hook, a high fade, an extra-high pitch, and so on. Take the appropriate club, try these different shots, and watch the results. When in trouble on the course you will deal with these creative situations much more effectively.

MASTER·STROKES

Use "Practice" Tempo On "Real" Shot

How many times have you seen a golfer make a smooth, rhythmic practice swing, followed by a fast, off-balance swing on the actual shot, with predictably poor results? Now think for a second: Is it possible that you're doing the same thing?

On the practice tee, rehearse making the tempo of your practice swing and your "real" swing identical. Before each shot, make a practice swing in which the back-swing and downswing are evenly paced, while you stay in good balance throughout. Then, step up to the ball and immediately duplicate this movement. Do this enough times in practice, and your "real" swing on the course will soon become smoother and much more effective.

MASTER STROKES

Work On Weaknesses After Round

The best time to practice is immediately after completing your round. This is when your mistakes will be fresh in your mind, and you can best work on specific corrections. Let's say you drove the ball poorly from the tee, but did other things well. Go to work on your tee shots. Review your errors and determine what caused them. Was your setup balanced? Your alignment square? Did you take the club away slowly and maintain a smooth rhythm? Did you maintain your balance, or did you lose balance by swinging too hard? Hit your shots in leisurely fashion as you check these possibilities. Chances are you'll spot the problem area, hit some good shots and regain your confidence.

OFF-COURSE TRAINING

It's unfortunately true that all the good advice about swinging the golf club has a limited value, if the player is physically incapable of executing the advice given. There's more that goes into a consistently powerful golf swing than most people realize. It requires high levels of strength, agility, balance, and coordination. That being the case, the following section covers some very basic suggestions on how to improve your body so that you then have the capacity to improve your golf swing.

Keep in mind that the exercises suggested here are deliberately kept simple and "do-able." They do not demand that you spend countless hours per week pumping iron in the gym. Most of them don't require you to go to a gym at all! And, many of them are written with older golfers in mind. It really is possible to regain some of the body tone of previous years, and with it, a more energetic and efficient golf swing.

Section 12:
CONTENTS

MASTER·STROKES

Rejuvenate In Off-Season

In most parts of the country, golfers must put away the clubs for at least a couple of months in the winter season. If you are intent on keeping your game at its current level with each succeeding year, make it a vow to use your off-season time to get your body in better shape for the next season. Work on exercises that in particular will build your abdominal muscles and your legs, and which will increase your overall flexibility. These will prove extremely beneficial to your golf game when you tee it up at the beginning of the following season. And you'll simply feel better, too.

MASTER·STROKES

Build Your Leg Power

Much of the power you generate in the swing comes from the lower body, particularly on tee shots. But as you get older, muscle mass begins to decrease. And this mass will decrease most in the largest muscles, those of the thighs and hips, unless you do something to arrest the trend.

The golfer who makes the effort to build upper leg strength will, over time, gain a tremendous advantage in carrying his or her shots as far as possible. Visit a gym and discuss with a counselor the exercises and equipment needed to rebuild your leg power. You'll give your long game a big boost by making this commitment.

MASTER·STROKES

Swing A Weighted Club

It's important to keep your "golf muscles" strong as you age. One of the best ways is to swing a club with some added weight. Take an old driver or fairway wood and add a weighted "donut" or a clip-on weight you can attach to the club's hosel. Adding just six or eight ounces to the neck of the club is all you need.

Get in the habit of making 50 slow, relaxed swings per day with this weighted club, which takes less than 10 minutes. This will keep the muscles of you back limber, and add surprising strength to your hands and forearms. Result: swinging the club during regular play will seem effortless.

x50

MASTER STROKES

Build Your Hand Strength

Strength in the hands and wrists is a tremendous asset on the golf course. This is particularly true when you encounter a shot where the ball lies in rough that can slow down or even stop the club-head at impact, snuffing out the shot. The stronger your hands and wrists, the better you can control the ball out of difficult lies. So, make it a point to have a spring-like hand grip handy. Work with it often, with both hands, whenever you have some idle time. A little work on your hand strength every day will pay tremendous dividends to your shotmaking.

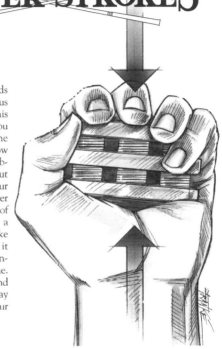

MASTER·STROKES

Walk Your Rounds

Far too many golfers have fallen into the lazy habit of riding in a cart every time they play golf. Doing so robs you of most of the exercise that is one of the greatest benefits of playing the game. Walking the five miles or so that an 18-hole round entails is great for virtually everybody. Not only is walking good for your heart, but you'll find that you'll gradually strengthen your legs as well, and this will definitely help you on your full swings. Finally, you'll find that if you play frequently, walking your rounds is an easy way to lose weight!

MASTER·STROKES

Strengthen Your Stomach

Most golfers don't think much of the importance of their stomach (abdominal) muscles. But strong abdominal muscles are necessary to help you turn fully away from and back through the ball, generating more power .

Do the following "stomach crunch" exercise: Lie on your back with feet flat and knees up. Extend both arms. Lift your head and shoulders slightly up from the floor and as you do so, reach both hands just above and to the left of your left knee. Drop back down, then lift again, this time reaching just beyond and to the right of your right knee. Start with 10 sets per day, then increase the number gradually. Soon you'll have a stronger and more flexible abdomen and a better turn.

MASTER·STROKES

Strengthen Left Fingers And Forearm

A common swing flaw is to relax the last two fingers of the left hand at the top of the backswing (insert). You must then re-grip the club on the way down, and you'll never re-grip exactly the same way. Errant shots result.

Here's an exercise to strengthen your left little finger and forearm. Take a heavy club like the sand wedge. Hook the end of the grip over your left little finger and underneath the butt of your hand. Hold the club straight out for as long as you can. (**Note:** If this is too heavy at first, hold the club farther down the grip.) Gradually increase the length of time you hold up the club. Do this exercise daily and you'll greatly increase your control of the club during the swing.

MASTER·STROKES

Sharpen Your Coordination

If you're not hitting your shots as solidly as you'd like, it could be that your coordination

needs sharpening. Here's a great coordination drill: Take your driver and a ball. Hold the club horizontally in front of you with your left hand about 10 inches from the neck of the club. Drop the ball onto the clubface and tap it upward as many times as you can, like a juggler. This will be difficult at first, but stay with it. As you improve the number of taps you can make, gradually move your hand farther from the clubhead. If you get to the point where you can control the ball with your hand on the grip itself, you'll also find yourself hitting the ball much more solidly!

MASTER·STROKES

Stretch The Torso

The more flexible you are in the mid-section, the better your turn will be away from and through the ball, and the more powerful your shots will be. Here's a good off-season exercise: Pick up an object that's fairly heavy, say 15 to 20 pounds, which you can hold in both arms. A medicine ball or a sack of flour or grass seed will suffice. Hold it in front of you while standing upright. Now turn your torso slowly to your right as far as you can. Return to center, hold, then slowly turn your torso to the left. Repeat 20 times per day. This exercise, which will take about five minutes, will add elasticity to your swing and trim down those "love handles" as well!

MASTER·STROKES

Build The Upper Legs

The largest muscles are in the upper legs, and as you age these muscles deteriorate. This means a gradual loss of stability and power in your swing. Here are two exercises you can do at home, without using weights:

1. For quadriceps (front of thigh) muscles, set your back against the wall, then move your feet out from the wall until you are in a "sitting" position. Hold for 30 seconds or until your quads are really "burning."

2. For hamstring (rear thigh) and gluteus (rear end) muscles, stand close to and facing a wall. Keeping your left leg straight, push it back as far as you can and return. Repeat 10 times with each leg.

MASTER·STROKES

SEATED
ROW →

Strengthen Your Back

Back problems are common among golfers, particularly seniors. Winter is a great time to strengthen your back muscles to prevent future injury. Here are two very good back exercises to work on at your local fitness center:

1. Seated Row: While sitting upright, grasp one handle in each hand and pull the handles toward you. The motion is as if rowing a boat; this works the upper back muscles.

2. Back Extension: Again starting from a sitting position, push backward against the resistance as far as you can; this strengthens the sensitive lower back. With both exercises, experiment to find the weight that allows you to do 12-15 repetitions without straining.

MASTER·STROKES

Small Snacks During Round

Are you a golfer who stops for 20 minutes after nine holes, gobbles a couple of hot dogs, some chips, and a beer or soda, then rushes out to the 10th tee? Not only is this unhealthy, but if you feel bloated for the next hour or two, your score on the back nine will be bloated, too.

You'll be much better off if you get in the habit of having multiple small, healthy snacks during the round. For example, eat a banana on the front nine, a small box of raisins or granola at the turn, and an apple later in the round. Also, make sure to drink plenty of water during play. Your health (and your score) will benefit from it.

MASTER·STROKES

Build Forearm Strength

Off-season is the time to improve yourself physically. Most seniors lose strength in the hands and forearms over the years. Here's a useful indoor exercise: Get a five-pound hand weight or barbell, and a short round bar. Tie a four-foot rope securely to both pieces. Hold the bar out in front of you at shoulder level. Wind the bar with both hands so the weight comes all the way up; then unwind it back down. Repeat three times for starters, then gradually increase the number of repetitions.

Do this for a few weeks and you'll increase your forearm strength greatly. On the course, you'll get the club through rough lies much better. Also, the club won't turn as much in your hands on mis-hit shots.

MASTER·STROKES

Exercise Your Left Shoulder

Over years of playing, your left shoulder takes a lot of wear and tear. It can become weaker and/or painful to play with. Here are two exercises to add strength and mobility to your left shoulder:

1. Stand facing a wall at arm's length. Walk your left hand up the wall as far as you can reach. Repeat several times.

2. Take a light weight in your left hand and lean over, keeping balance with your right hand on a desk or table. Make small clockwise circular movements with your left hand. Gradually make the circles larger. Slow to a stop, then repeat making circles in the opposite direction.

YOUR EQUIPMENT

The implements with which golfers play have changed dramatically in the last decade or two. On the whole, the development of larger clubheads, lighter materials, a much greater choice of club shafts, and much more consistent golf balls have combined to make the game much easier to play.

However, there are many more choices to be made regarding equipment than in years past. And, the golfer must make the right choices for his or her game in order to benefit from improved equipment technology. This section will help guide you in making these choices. In addition, you'll find some good tips regarding maintaining your equipment, an area in which the average amateur is notoriously lax. Keeping your equipment in the best possible shape so it can do the job it was designed for, can only help your game.

Section 13:

CONTENTS

MASTER·STROKES

Use the Right Shaft Flex

Golf is a lot tougher if you are using clubs that are too "strong" for your athletic level, either in terms of total weight or shaft flex. If you're playing the same clubs you used many years ago, their shaft flex may now be too stiff for you. Here's a telltale sign: If your shots consistently fly too low and tend to slide right, chances are you need more flexible clubshafts. The bottom of a shaft with more flex will actually bend forward more at impact; this serves to deliver the clubface to the ball with slightly more loft, as well as to square up the clubface rather than leaving it open. Experiment with some "softer" shafts and you'll see the difference.

FLEX POINT

MASTER STROKES

Are Your Clubs Too Upright?

The lie of the club, meaning the angle at which the shaft enters the clubhead, is an often-overlooked clubfitting factor. If the lie is incorrect, the sole won't sit flush to the ground. This contributes to poor contact.

For reasons too complex to describe here, many manufacturers make clubs with more "upright" lies than in the past. If the lie is too upright, it means the toe will be off the ground. This isn't a big problem with a driver where you're hitting off a tee. But it is a problem with all other clubs. To check your lie, take your address on a linoleum floor. Have someone slip a sheet of paper under the sole of the club. A little "breathing room" under the toe is okay, but if the paper reaches beyond the center of the clubface, the lie is too upright.

LIE TOO UPRIGHT

OK

MASTER·STROKES

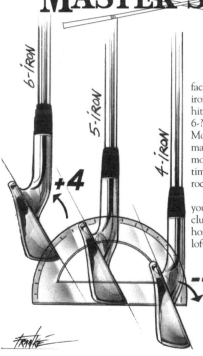

Check Your Iron Lofts

Have you ever been puzzled by the fact that you hit, say, your 6- and 7-irons the same distance? Or that you hit your 5-iron a lot farther than your 6-? The fault is probably not yours. More likely, your iron lofts are off. This may occur due to manufacturer error; more often, your iron lofts change over time as you hit shots off hard ground, rocks, roots, or other obstacles.

Winter is a good time to have your lofts checked by a professional club repairer. If any are off, the club's hosel can be bent slightly to return the loft to normal. You want a difference in loft of 4 degrees between each iron club, no less than 3 1/2. This assures you'll get uniform differences in the distances you hit each club.

MASTER STROKES

Consider Longer Driver

The longer the "lever" you swing, the more centrifugal force you'll apply to the end of the lever (the clubhead). And all other things being equal, you'll gain approximately five yards in tee-shot length for every inch longer the shaft of your driver is.

Before rushing out and buying an ultra-long club, however, remember that every golfer has a limit to the length of club they can consistently return squarely to the ball. Experiment with a driver that's just one inch longer than what you're used to. Don't go longer than that until you've proved to yourself you are still hitting the ball solidly and with control.

MASTER·STROKES

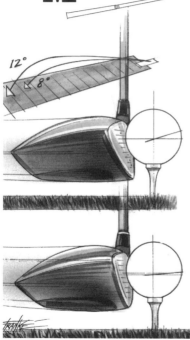

Optimize Driver Launch Angle

To get as much carry as possible from your tee shots, it's important to obtain the proper launch angle on your drives. You may need to launch your tee shots at a little higher angle. If the ball leaves the tee at a very low angle, say eight degrees, it must have a great deal of velocity to get the maximum possible carry. If you don't generate as much clubhead speed as in the past, you may need to launch the ball a little higher, say at 12 or 13 degrees, to obtain your greatest carry distance.

Experiment on the practice tee with some higher-lofted drivers and observe your flight and total carry. You may find some surprising and pleasant results!

MASTER·STROKES

Use the Right Sand Wedge

The sand wedge's design and thus its performance can vary greatly. You should know particularly how the sole or flange affects your shots, both out of sand traps and also off grass.

If the flange is wide and has a lot of "bounce," meaning the rear of the flange is much lower than the leading edge, the clubhead will tend to skid or bounce through sand rather than dig deeply. This makes it the choice if your course has greenside bunkers with soft, deep sand. If the sand is firmer, or if there aren't many bunkers and you use the club often from fairway lies, less bounce makes it easier to hit these shots cleanly. Choose a sand wedge to match the shots you'll play most often.

MASTER·STROKES

Carry The 7-Wood

The long irons (2, 3 and 4) require substantial clubhead speed and a near-perfect angle of attack to obtain a desirable flight. Many seniors have found adding a 7-wood to their set and taking out a long iron very helpful. Although the 7-wood has about the same loft as a 3-iron, its shallower clubface allows you to meet the ball slightly below its center of gravity. This adds lift to the shot, even if you don't catch it "pure." Also, the 7-wood's broader sole makes it a much easier club to hit out of the rough, since the sole "flattens" the grass just before impact so the clubhead meets less resistance.

MASTER·STROKES

"Too Thick"

Check Your Grip Size

If you struggle with a slice, it may be because of your equipment. If your grips are too thick, this will impede your wrist release through impact, making it difficult to square up the clubface at impact.

Check your grip diameter by holding the club in your left hand. Do the tips of your middle and third fingers brush against the pad of your thumb? If they don't and there's a visible space, it means the grip is too large for your hands. Have your clubs re-gripped with less tape wound under the grips, thus reducing their diameter.

MASTER·STROKES

Use The Right Length Putter

Many golfers experiment with different putters. Most concern themselves with factors such as the head's shape, the weight, or the feel at impact. Consider also whether the club's length is right for you. (Most men's putters are 34, 35 or 36 inches; women's models usually range 1 inch shorter.) If anything, the majority will err toward a putter that's too long. This can cause you to feel cramped at address and during the stroke, because your hands and forearms are hunched rather than hanging freely. Experiment with a putter that's just 1 inch shorter, and you might be surprised by the improved comfort at address and during the stroke.

MASTER STROKES

Tale Of The (Impact) Tape

There's a reason good golfers consistently hit accurate shots: They strike the ball at or near the center of the clubface.

How precisely do you strike the ball? There's a way to find out. Get some impact tape, available in most golf pro shops or retail outlets. Place the tape on your clubface (a teed-up driver or 3-wood is best), then hit shots on the practice tee. With each shot, the ball will leave a mark at the point of contact. Thus it gives you feedback as to how far off-center you're hitting your shots, and toward what part of the clubface (toe, heel, top or bottom). Keep hitting practice shots while observing your point of impact. You'll gradually learn to adjust toward a more solid impact.

MASTER·STROKES

"Hotter" Balls Affect Your Short Game

Companies promote golf balls that promise to go farther than ever. This is attractive to most amateurs, especially seniors who need extra yardage. But keep this in mind: The "hotter" the ball is off the tee, the hotter it will also be around the greens. "Longer" balls don't come off the clubface with as much backspin as you may be accustomed to. They will land at a shallower angle and with less backspin, and thus will roll farther upon landing.

If you play a "hot" ball, know that you must adjust on short game shots. Practice with the ball to see just how much farther your chips, pitches and sand shots tend to roll upon landing, and on the course, allow for it whenever possible.

HOT BALL!

←HIGH SPIN BALL

MASTER·STROKES

Lighten Your (Shaft) Load

As you age, clubs that were easy to swing 20 years ago may now feel a bit heavy. If so, you'll find it difficult to hit the ball on a high trajectory and will lose a little distance.

For seniors, lighter shafts can be a great benefit. Today many light-weight steel shafts are available, and graphite shafts are even lighter. While regular steel shafts weigh some 4 1/4 ounces, lightweight steel weighs about 3 1/2 ounces. Graphite shafts have a wide weight range, with most between 2 1/2 and 3 ounces. Reducing shaft weight makes swinging the club much easier. **Note:** You'll need to practice with lighter shafts to adjust your timing and be comfortable with them on the course.

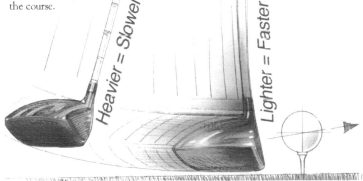

Heavier = Slower

Lighter = Faster

MASTER·STROKES

Find Putter Sweet Spot

To putt their best, most golfers think about reading the green correctly, aligning the putterface properly, and keeping the stroke on line. All these are important. But don't forget the most important element of all: Hitting the ball on the putter's center of percussion, or "sweet spot."

To find the sweet spot, hold your putter vertically, and tap the face with a tee. Keep tapping until you find the spot at which the putterface rebounds straight back with no vibration. This is the spot you should strive to make contact with on every putt. If you can do this, you'll get the truest possible roll, every time.

MASTER STROKES

Check Your Wedge Lofts

Many amateurs assume equal spacing in lofts between all clubs (roughly four degrees apart). This is usually not true of the wedges. Most of today's pitching wedges have less loft than in the past, perhaps 44 to 46 degrees of loft. Meanwhile, most sand wedges have 56 degrees. So you may have a difference of up to 12 degrees of loft between these two clubs, way too large a "gap."

Check the lofts of your wedges. If the gap is eight degrees or more, either have the lofts bent slightly to reduce the gap; or, add a "mid" or "gap" wedge with a loft midway between your sand wedge and pitching wedge. Wedge lofts that are four degrees apart will simplify your short game shot choices.

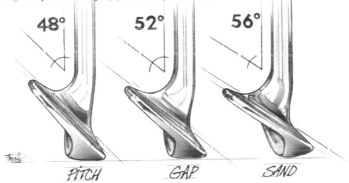

48°   52°   56°

PITCH   GAP   SAND

MASTER·STROKES

How Club's Lie Affects Shots

The lie refers to the angle at which the clubshaft enters the clubhead. If the lie is correct, the sole of the club should be flat at address and through impact.

If the club's lie is too upright for you, the toe of the club will be raised up off the ground (this is the more common lie error). This causes the heel to catch the ground at impact, closing the clubface. The result is a shot that is pulled or smothered to the left. If the club's lie is too flat, the toe touches the ground while the heel is up. This will open the clubface at impact, leading to weak shots that fly to the right. Have a clubfitter check your clubs' lies—it's a good investment in improved shotmaking.

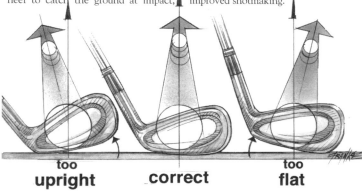

too
upright   **correct**   **too**
flat

MASTER·STROKES

Check Your Putter Lie

Quite a few amateurs use a putter that's fine except for one thing: The lie is not flat to the surface when they're in their normal stroking position.

Most often, the putter lie is too upright (meaning the heel is down and the toe in the air). This can cause three problems. First, you may catch the putter during the takeaway, disrupting stroke rhythm and clubface angle. Second, you may scuff the ground through impact, slowing the face and closing it so you miss left. Third is the little-known fact that when the club rests on the heel, the slight loft makes the putterface aim slightly left of where you think. So when you select a putter, make sure the sole rests flat at address. You'll make more putts.

PUTTER
ON
HEEL

MASTER·STROKES

Use Softer Grips

Many older golfers are hampered by the onset of arthritis in the joints, particularly the hands and fingers. It can become difficult to get a good grip and feel for the club, particularly in chilly weather.

If your hands bother you during play, consider switching to grips designed for golfers with arthritic problems. Basically, arthritic grips are made from compounds that are substantially softer than standard grips, providing a much more cushiony feel. Most major grip manufacturers produce a soft or arthritic grip. Ask to see them at your pro shop or retail outlet. The change will provide you with greater comfort and control of the club as well.

softer
thicker

MASTER·STROKES

The 3-Wood Tee Shot

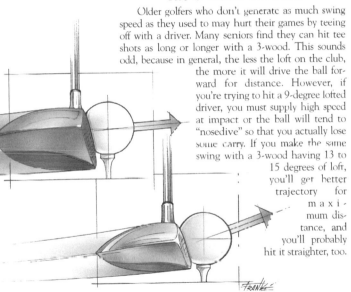

Older golfers who don't generate as much swing speed as they used to may hurt their games by teeing off with a driver. Many seniors find they can hit tee shots as long or longer with a 3-wood. This sounds odd, because in general, the less the loft on the club, the more it will drive the ball forward for distance. However, if you're trying to hit a 9-degree lofted driver, you must supply high speed at impact or the ball will tend to "nosedive" so that you actually lose some carry. If you make the same swing with a 3-wood having 13 to 15 degrees of loft, you'll get better trajectory for maximum distance, and you'll probably hit it straighter, too.

MASTER·STROKES

Consider Heavier Putter

If your putting stroke seems quick and nervous and nothing will drop, consider this move: Try a putter with a noticeably heavier head weight. A heavier putter will automatically slow your stroke to some degree. It will also make it easier for you to keep the club low to the ground rather than snatching it up on the backstroke. The result will be a more even tempo with the clubhead moving levelly at impact and imparting a smoother roll to the ball. Try out a heavier putter on the practice green and see if you don't regain your stroke and your confidence.

MASTER·STROKES

Keep Your Grips Clean

A large majority of amateurs make the game harder through a very simple omission: They rarely if ever clean the grips on their clubs. Over time, dirt and perspiration build up on grips so they lose their tacky feel. When your grips are slick, whether you realize it or not, you must hold on tighter so that you lose clubhead speed and freedom in your swing.

All you need to do is this: Rub your grips with a towel dipped in warm soapy water, then dry them thoroughly. Clean your grips after every three rounds and you'll feel the difference every time you pick up a club. Finally, if you play once or more per week, replace your grips at least after every two seasons.

MASTER·STROKES

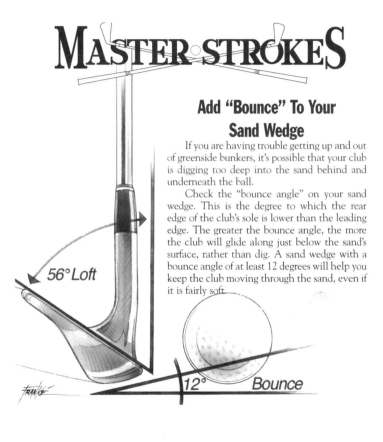

Add "Bounce" To Your Sand Wedge

If you are having trouble getting up and out of greenside bunkers, it's possible that your club is digging too deep into the sand behind and underneath the ball.

Check the "bounce angle" on your sand wedge. This is the degree to which the rear edge of the club's sole is lower than the leading edge. The greater the bounce angle, the more the club will glide along just below the sand's surface, rather than dig. A sand wedge with a bounce angle of at least 12 degrees will help you keep the club moving through the sand, even if it is fairly soft.

56° Loft

12° Bounce

MASTER·STROKES

Check Putter Loft

Most golfers don't realize it, but the face of the putter has some loft on it — usually between two and six degrees. The reason is that the ball needs just a bit of "lift" to get it rolling along the top of the grass blades.

If the greens you play on are slow and bumpy, it helps to have a putter with a little more loft. On smooth, close-cut greens, less loft is needed. If you notice that your putts are not getting off to a smooth start, you might want to have a professional check the loft on your putter. If necessary, the loft can usually be adjusted by a degree or two either way. Giving your putts a smoother start will help you make more in the long run.

**Low
Loft
Smooth
Green**

**High
Loft
Rough
Green**

MASTER·STROKES

A Good Time To Re-Grip

Many amateurs are lax about maintaining their equipment. Perhaps the biggest fault is failing to re-grip their clubs regularly.

Although you may not realize it, playing with slick, worn-out grips hurts your game. They force you to hold on tighter throughout the swing. You end up losing both club-head speed and control.

So, remember to re-grip your clubs regularly. A good rule of thumb is to re-grip after every season if you play and practice a lot; or after every two seasons if you play, say, 25-40 times per year.

MASTER·STROKES

Keep Spikes Clean

Most golfer now wear "soft" golf spikes with short plastic nubs as opposed to steel spikes. While the soft spikes help the condition of the course, they do not offer quite as much traction during the swing. Usually there's no problem. However, it's easy for soft spikes to get filled with grass or dirt during play. This can cause slippage and loss of balance during full swings, which is of particular concern for seniors (both in terms of the result of the shot and possible injury!) So, especially in wet conditions, check your soft spikes at the tee. If they're clogged, use the shoe brushes that are sometimes available on the tee, or clean out the dirt with a ball-mark repair tool. Better footing (and better shots) will result.

The Rule
of Golf

RULES OF THE GAME

How well do you really know the rules? If you're like most amateurs, probably not well enough. There are 34 basic Rules of Golf. However, there are so many permutations to those rules that there are literally hundreds, and perhaps thousands, of questions that can come up in the course of a round of golf. Certainly they won't all come up during one round. Over several seasons, though, most or all of the items that are covered in this extensive section, will come up, either for yourself or within your foursome. So do yourself a favor and familiarize yourself with all of these rules situations. Knowing the correct rulings may save you a stroke or two during an important competition, or at least, save you from errors that result in penalties or disqualification. And, you can take pride in being a golfer who "knows the rules."

CONTENTS

MASTER·STROKES

Putt Can't Hit Flagstick

If your ball is on the green, when you putt do one of two things: Either remove the flag from the hole or, if you have a long putt and want the flag left in to aid depth perception, ask a playing partner to attend the flag and pull it out immediately after you stroke your putt. If you putt from on the putting surface and the ball hits the flag, it's a two-stroke penalty.

Whenever the ball is off the green, you may play your shot while leaving the flagstick in. If the ball hits it, there's no penalty. This includes any shots you play with the putter when the ball is a short distance off the green.

MASTER·STROKES

Know Your Teeing Area

Many amateurs tee up only on a line between the tee markers. But the rules define the teeing area as a rectangle as wide as the distance between the tee markers, and two full club-lengths back from them. This gives you an area of more than seven feet behind the markers. And, only the ball needs to be within this rectangle—you don't have to be!

Using the entire area helps you in two ways: 1) Tees are never dead flat. You can find a spot that slopes a little uphill, downhill or sidehill to assist in getting a certain desired flight; 2) On par-3s, if you're "between clubs," you can drop back two driver lengths, go with the longer club, swing smoothly and hit it closer to the hole.

MASTER·STROKES

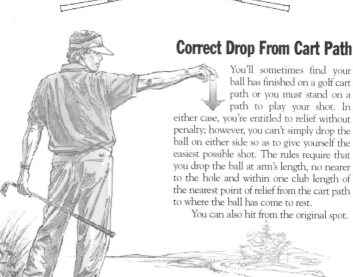

Correct Drop From Cart Path

You'll sometimes find your ball has finished on a golf cart path or you must stand on a path to play your shot. In either case, you're entitled to relief without penalty; however, you can't simply drop the ball on either side so as to give yourself the easiest possible shot. The rules require that you drop the ball at arm's length, no nearer to the hole and within one club length of the nearest point of relief from the cart path to where the ball has come to rest.

You can also hit from the original spot.

MASTER·STROKES

Options For The Unplayable Lie

You've hit into bushes which make it impossible to play the ball out. You must take an unplayable-lie penalty of one stroke. But remember when taking an unplayable lie, you have not one but three options: 1) Move the ball two club-lengths to either side, with the ball no closer to the hole; 2) If this doesn't get you clear, you may move the ball back from the hole as far as you wish, but you must make sure to keep the point where the ball came to rest between yourself and the hole; 3) If this also doesn't leave you with a shot, you may go back to the spot of your original stroke and replay it from there, again taking a one-shot penalty.

MASTER·STROKES

Playing The Wrong Ball

You walk out to the vicinity where you've hit your drive, then play your shot. Only at the green do you realize you played the wrong ball on your second shot.

The penalty for playing the wrong ball is loss of the hole if you're playing a match, and two strokes in regular stroke play. It's a penalty you never want to incur.

So, do the following: Always know what brand and type of ball you are playing; put a small mark on the ball before you begin play so you can identify it, even if someone else in your group is playing the same model; and always, always, look at the ball you're sure is "yours" before you play your next shot.

MASTER·STROKES

How To Mark The Ball Correctly

Many newer golfers are uncertain about how to mark their ball (the Rules of Golf allow you to mark, lift and clean the ball once it's on the putting surface).

To correctly mark your ball, take a small- to moderate-sized coin and place it immediately behind the ball's position. (When we say "behind" the ball, we mean at the rear of the ball as it relates to the hole.) You may then pick the ball up. Many golfers are under the impression that the coin must be "stuffed" underneath the ball, on the spot where it actually came to rest. This is unnecessary. When it's time to putt, simply place the ball immediately in front of the coin, then pick up the coin.

MASTER·STROKES

The Out-of-Bounds Penalty

When you hit a ball out of bounds, meaning outside the boundaries of the course as defined by white stakes, the rule is clear: Play a second ball from the same spot as your first stroke, adding a stroke penalty. In other words, if your tee shot finishes out of bounds, you must count the stroke, add a penalty stroke, then play another shot from the tee, which would count as your third stroke on the hole.

It's always wise, if you're uncertain whether your shot has gone out of bounds, to hit a provisional ball from the original spot. This way if your first ball did finish out of bounds, you don't have to go all the way back to replay it.

MASTER·STROKES

Shot Off Green Hits Ball On Green

Your shot from off the green lands and hits a ball resting on the green. Under the rules, what must be done? In this case, you play your ball from where it came to rest, with no penalty. The player whose ball has been moved, however, must replace it as near as possible to its original position. If it isn't replaced, the player incurs a two-stroke penalty in stroke play, or loss of hole in match play.

What if your putted ball from on the green hits someone else's ball? In this case, the other player would again replace his or her ball, but you would receive a two-stroke penalty. So if anyone else's ball is near your line, ask them to mark it!

ORIGINAL POSITION

MASTER·STROKES

Ball On Lip: How Long Can You Wait?

You've just hit a great putt; it takes the break and curls right toward the hole, only to stop tantalizingly on the lip. You wait anxiously, hoping for it to drop.

According to the rules, just how long can you wait?

Once you've hit the putt, you're expected to walk to the hole without any undue delay. When you've reached your ball and the hole, you may wait a maximum of 10 seconds to see if the ball will drop in. If you delay any longer than that, under the rules, you must take a one-stroke penalty.

MASTER STROKES

Penalty For Too Many Clubs

Many golfers have become infatuated with the latest golf equipment technology and have bought new drivers, extra fairway woods and wedges. Some forget just how many clubs are in their bag at any time!

If you are playing in any organized event (or even in a match within your weekly foursome), you may carry a maximum of 14 clubs. The penalty for carrying more than 14 clubs is as follows: In stroke play, it is two strokes for each hole that the error occurred, with a maximum penalty of four strokes. In match play, the penalty is loss of one hole if the error is discovered after the first hole played, or a maximum of two holes if the mistake is discovered later.

MASTER·STROKES

Ball In A Rain-Filled Bunker

If you play after a rainstorm, you'll sometimes find your ball resting in standing water within a sand bunker. If so, the rules are as follows: You are allowed, with no penalty, to lift the ball from the water and drop it at the nearest point within the bunker that provides relief. However, if the entire bunker is filled with water so that you can't obtain relief within it, you may drop the ball outside the bunker, keeping the point at which the ball entered the bunker between yourself and the hole. However, in this case, there is a penalty of one stroke.

Keep in mind that you always have the option of playing the ball from where it originally rested in the bunker.

MASTER·STROKES

Forgetting To Replace Moved Marker

When your ball is near the line of another player's putt, you mark its spot by placing a small coin behind it. Sometimes, when your coin is directly on the other player's line, you'll need to move the coin, usually by measuring one or two putterhead widths to one side of the ball and placing your coin there.

Remember that under the rules you are responsible for moving your coin and the ball back to its original spot before you putt. If you forget, the penalty is one stroke. A good tip: Whenever you mark a ball and do not have to move it to the side, place the coin "heads up." For those times when you must move it sideways, after moving the coin, place it "tails up." When it's your turn to putt, this will remind you that you must move your coin back.

LINE OF PUTT

MASTER·STROKES

How Long Can You Look?

You're playing in a match and you've hit your tee shot into the woods. Although you have a good idea where it came to rest, when you arrive in the area, you don't see a ball. How long do you have to look for it before you must decide it is lost and take a penalty? According to the rules, you have five minutes from the moment you (or your partner or your caddie) reach the area where you think your ball has stopped. If you don't find it within that period, you must go back to the tee and play another ball, at a penalty of one stroke plus distance.

MASTER·STROKES

Don't Break The Limbs

Occasionally you'll find yourself in a predicament off the fairway where your ball is lying cleanly, but your backswing is impeded by a single limb or part of a bush. Keep in mind that the Rules of Golf do not allow a player to either move, bend or break anything that is growing or fixed in the course of playing a shot. Remember that this means that you not only can't actually break off part of a living plant, but you can't use your body to deliberately bend it or step on it so that it is out of the way of your swing. Penalty for violating rule is two strokes in stroke play, loss of hole in match play.

MASTER·STROKES

DROP

CLEAN

LIFT

Embedded Ball Rule

Sometimes in wet conditions, you'll find your tee shot or approach shot has embedded or "plugged" — that is, landed and stopped in its own pitch mark. The rules state that if you find that your ball is embedded in any closely mown area of the course, but not in a hazard, you are entitled to lift and clean the ball with no penalty. Then you must drop the ball as near as possible to the spot where it landed, but no closer to the hole.

MASTER STROKES

Don't Point Out Putting Line

According to the Rules of Golf, prior to putting, it is allowable for your partner or caddie to point out or suggest the line of roll that your putt may be expected to take (without actually touching the green). However, once you are over the ball (that is, in the act of putting) no player or caddie can continue to point out the expected line of roll, or mark that line in any way. Penalty for breach of this rule is two strokes in stroke play, and loss of hole in match play.

MASTER·STROKES

Can You Clean the Ball?

Fairly often, especially in damp conditions, your ball will pick up some mud upon landing. According to the Rules of Golf, the only time you may pick up and clean the ball, aside from when it has become embedded in its own pitch mark, is after it has reached the putting surface. In all other situations, you must play the ball as it lies. However, once you've gotten to the green, always mark, clean and replace the ball to give you the best possible chance at obtaining a true roll.

MASTER·STROKES

Can You Move the Twig?

Your ball has come to rest in the woods and you've found that you have a clear swing. However, the ball has a small twig lying against the front of it. Are you allowed to move the twig away from the ball?

A twig is classified as a loose impediment. When your ball is not lying in a hazard, as in this case, you may remove a loose impediment from the area of the ball without penalty. However, keep in mind that if in removing the impediment the ball should move, you will incur a one-stroke penalty. If it seems likely that moving the twig will move the ball, don't take the risk: Don't move the twig.

MASTER·STROKES

When Is Ball Out Of Bounds?

Your opponent hits a tee shot that lands perilously close to out-of-bounds markers. When you reach the ball, you line its position up with the white stakes marking the course boundary line. As best you can determine, most but not all of the ball is outside of a line defined by the inside of the boundary stakes. You tell your opponent that the ball is "out," but he insists he can play it. Who is correct?

Your opponent is. According to the rules, all of the ball must rest outside the boundary stakes for the ball to be deemed out of bounds. The player may continue with no penalty.

MASTER·STROKES

Club Hits Ball Twice

When playing a greenside recovery from deep rough, you hit the shot "fat" so that the ball pops up weakly. As you follow through, the clubhead taps the ball again so that it veers off to the left. Is there any penalty?

This problem occurs most often on short shots where the speed of the clubhead, slow to begin with, can be snuffed completely by heavy grass. If this happens, you must count a total of two strokes, one for each time the clubhead contacted the ball, and then play the ball from where it came to rest.

MASTER·STROKES

Can You Play from Cart Path?

You've hit your tee shot off line to the right, and it's come to rest on the right side of a paved cart path. You are entitled to relief from the path without penalty.

However, since you must drop the ball within one club length at the nearest point of relief, in this case you would need to drop to the right of the path. This would put your ball in rough, and also, you would be more likely to hit the trees in front of you.

Keep in mind that while you are entitled to a free drop from paved cart paths, you may also play the ball as it lies, when taking the drop would put you in a more difficult position.

MASTER·STROKES

Player Must Move Before Shot Is Played.

Indicating Line On Blind Shot

Occasionally you will face a blind shot over a hill (usually from near the green) so that you cannot see the position of the flag. In such cases, it is allowable to ask another player to indicate the line to the flag prior to playing the shot. However, he or she may not stand on that line as you actually play the shot; nor may they leave an object on the ground to mark the line of the shot as you play it.

Keep in mind that you may also authorize a playing partner to lift the flagstick up from the hole in order to allow you to see the top of it, and thus estimate the hole's position.

MASTER STROKES

Conceding Opponent's Putt

THAT'S GOOD.

You and your partner are in a match against two other players. One of your opponents has a putt of less than two feet to tie the hole. Your partner says, "That's good," meaning the putt is conceded. The opponent, instead of picking up the ball, taps it carelessly and misses. You claim that since your opponent elected to putt the ball and missed, that your side has won the hole. Is this correct?

No. According to the rules, a player may concede that an opponent has holed out with his or her next stroke at any time. Once this concession has been stated, it may not be withdrawn, nor may the opponent decline it. In this case, the hole is tied.

MASTER·STROKES

Grounding Club In Sand Trap

Many amateurs, particularly those relatively new to the game, are unaware of many rules involving hazards on the course. One of the most common violations involves sand. Whenever your ball is resting in a sand trap, you may not ground the club right behind the ball, but must instead hover the club above the sand. Grounding the club in effect improves the lie because you are pressing down on the sand behind the ball. Also keep in mind that the clubhead may not brush the sand as you begin the backswing. The penalty for grounding the club in a trap is two strokes in stroke play, loss of hole in match play.

MASTER·STROKES

"What Club Did You Hit?"

There are many occasions, particularly on tee shots on par-threes, where knowing what club your opponent hit may be useful information in deciding what club to hit yourself. Keep in mind, however, that the rules prohibit you from asking any opponent what club he or she hit. The penalty for asking such advice is loss of hole in match play or two strokes in stroke play. Keep in mind that if you are playing with a partner, you are free to discuss with him or her what club to select.

MASTER·STROKES

Removing Out-of-Bounds Stake

Your tee shot, which you feared was out-of-bounds, instead has come to rest just in bounds. The bad news is that the ball is nearly against one of the white stakes that marks the boundary. Is it okay to remove the stake to allow you a clear swing?

Unfortunately, no. The rules prohibit the removal of boundary stakes for the purpose of making an unimpeded swing. You must either advance the ball as best you can with a swing impeded by the stake; or you may declare the ball unplayable and move it, under a one-stroke penalty. Breach of this rule calls for loss of hole in match play, two strokes in stroke play.

MASTER·STROKES

Signing Incorrect Scorecard

In a tournament, after finishing your round, you forget to carefully study your hole-by-hole scores which were marked down by a fellow competitor. He inadvertently wrote an incorrect score for your 18th hole; you sign for the card as marked. What happens?

No matter what, you will lose out. If the score you signed for is lower than what you actually shot, the penalty is disqualification. If the score you signed for is higher than your real score, you must accept the higher score as marked on the card. So, always check each hole on your scorecard before signing it and turning it in!

MASTER·STROKES

Ball Moves At Address

Your ball is sitting "up" in the rough. You address the ball, setting the clubhead behind it, and as you do so the ball moves. Any time the ball has moved from its original position while you are addressing it, you must take a penalty of one stroke.

Remember that when you find the ball in a lie in which it's above the ground's surface, such as when it's resting on pine needles or perched up in rough, it can easily be moved by merely setting your club on the ground behind it. When you have such a lie, make it a habit to hover your club just above the ground behind the ball, assuring you don't incur a penalty.

MASTER STROKES

Free Drop Moves Ball From Rough

Your ball comes to rest a few feet off the green in the rough, but atop a sprinkler head. You say you are entitled to a free drop within one club length of the nearest point of relief, no closer to the hole. Your opponent agrees. However, when you move the ball to this point of relief, you can drop the ball on the close-cut apron of the green, from where you can putt it. Your opponent objects, saying you must drop the ball in the rough. Is this correct?

No. The rules do not differentiate between "rough" and the fairway or the green's apron. All these areas are simply considered "through the green." As long as you drop at the spot that provides the nearest relief from the obstruction for your stance and swing, the ball can be dropped on close-cut grass rather than in the rough.

MASTER·STROKES

No

Yes

Dropping Ball Incorrectly

When you are taking a drop during the course of play, either a free drop or one in which you are incurring a penalty, you must drop the ball in the manner prescribed by the rules. To drop correctly at the determined spot, stand erect with your arm extended fully at shoulder height, and drop the ball so that it lands without touching you. If you fail to drop the ball correctly, you may lift and drop the ball again without penalty. However, if you fail to make the drop in the correct manner and go on to play your shot, the penalty is one stroke.

MASTER·STROKES

Changing Club's Makeup During Play

Is it all right to change the playing characteristics of a club during a round? Say you have a driver to which you have added lead tape on the clubhead, to simply add weight or, by placing it toward either the heel or the toe, to alter the center of gravity of the clubhead. You decide after several holes of a round in your club championship that the club feels extra heavy today. So you remove the lead strips, figuring it will give the clubhead a better feel for the remainder of the round. You use the driver on the next hole.

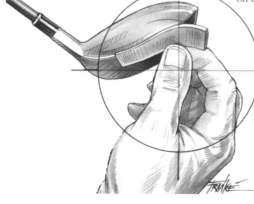

A legal move? Absolutely not. Removing the lead tape constitutes a change in the playing characteristics of the club during the round, and the penalty for this is disqualification!

MASTER·STROKES

Don't Repair Spike Marks

Despite the increased use of "soft" versus metal golf spikes, golfers still often encounter raised spike marks along the line of putt. Is it permissible to tap down spike marks in your line?

No. The rules state that, unlike with ball marks that you may repair, marks made by spiked golf shoes along your line may not be tapped down. Penalty for breach of this rule is two strokes in stroke play and loss of hole in match play. Final note: It is allowable, and good etiquette, to tap down spike marks after play of the hole is completed.

MASTER·STROKES

Replacing a Damaged Club

During a competitive round, you fumble your putter as you try to remove it from your golf cart. Surprisingly, it hits the cement cart path at such an angle that the shaft snaps just below the clubhead. What do the rules allow you to do?

If the putter (or any club) is accidentally damaged during play, the rules state that you may replace it with another club, although the replacement may not be a club being used by another player on the course. Also, any replacement must be made without unduly delaying play.

Note: If you deliberately damage or break a club during play, you may not replace it during the round.

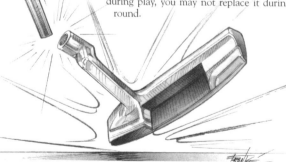

MASTER·STROKES

Unplayable Lie In Bunker

Your approach shot has embedded itself in the lip of a sand bunker, just above the sand itself. You decide that the ball is unplayable. What must you do?

First, keep in mind that the ball would be deemed within the bunker, which is a hazard. You have three options, each of which calls for a penalty of one stroke:

1. Play the ball from as near as possible to the spot of your previous stroke.

2. Drop within two club lengths of the spot where the ball lies, no closer to the hole.

3. Drop any distance behind where the ball came to rest, keeping that point between you and the hole.

Keep in mind, however, that if you choose either the second or third option, you must drop the ball in the bunker, not outside it

MASTER·STROKES

Can You Repair Damaged Hole?

Upon reaching the green, you notice that one side of the hole has been damaged in some way so that it appears dented in. You attempt to repair the hole, pushing back on the inside of the hole to remove the dent so that the hole more closely resembles a perfect circle. Is anything wrong with this?

Yes! According to the rules, you may not repair any damage to the putting green (of which the hole itself is a part) if such repair might assist your play of the hole.

The penalty is two strokes in stroke play, loss of hole in match play. **Note:** You may try to repair the hole once play of the hole is completed.

MASTER STROKES

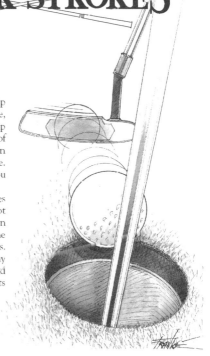

Tapping In With Pin In

You've just hit a wonderful chip shot to within 18 inches of the hole, a virtual "gimme" par. You walk up to the ball and, to get it out of everyone's way, quickly tap it in while the flagstick is in the hole. Your opponent says, "I'm afraid you lose the hole." Is she correct?

Unfortunately, yes. The rules state that a player's ball must not strike an unattended flagstick when the stroke has been played from the putting surface, as this one was. Penalty is loss of hole in match play and two strokes in stroke play, and the ball must be re-played from its original position on the green.

MASTER·STROKES

Ball Moves From Original Spot On Green

On a breezy day, you mark the position of your ball on the green with a coin. When it's your turn, you replace the ball and pick up the coin. After reading your putt but prior to taking your stance, you see that the ball has moved from its original position. Must you take a penalty stroke?

In this case, the answer is no. You have not caused the ball to move by making contact with it; nor did you have your feet in position to play the stroke with your clubhead "grounded" behind the ball when it moved. You may play your next shot with no penalty from where the ball now rests.

MASTER STROKES

Second Ball Impedes Your Shot

You and your opponent in match play hit good drives. You find his ball lying a foot in front of yours in the fairway. You ask him to lift his ball since your ball might hit it just as it takes off. He says that under the rules he may not move his ball. Who is right?

You are. If the opponent's ball in any way impedes your swing or stance, the opponent must lift his ball if requested, then replace it at the marked spot. In stroke play, the golfer whose ball is impeding the other ball may opt to play his ball first, rather than lift it.

MASTER STROKES

Your Shot Hits You

You're trying to punch a recovery from the woods. Just after you make contact, the ball hits a root in front of you and ricochets up, striking you on the arm and dropping a short distance away. You play another shot to get out to the fairway. As you approach your ball another member of your foursome says, "You have to take a penalty." Is he right?

Yes, he is. In stroke play, if the ball is deflected or stopped by yourself (or by your caddie or your equipment), the penalty is two strokes. In match play, if the ball hits you (or your partner, your caddie or your equipment) the penalty is loss of hole.

MASTER·STROKES

What is Your Handicap?

If you are a casual golfer, you may not have an established handicap. Here's how to compute one:

1. Record scores for 20 rounds, along with the course rating from the tees played from.

2. Subtract course rating from score (for example, 92 - 70.5 = 21.5.) **3.** Take the 10 best scores (lowest amounts above the course ratings). Add these numbers and divide by 10. Then multiply this number by 96 percent.

Example: Your 10 best of 20 scores total 177 strokes above the course ratings. Divide by 10: You average 17.7 strokes above the course rating per round. Multiply 17.7 by 96 percent; your current handicap is 17.0. Keep adding future rounds and deleting oldest scores to keep your handicap current.

MASTER·STROKES

Puddle Between Ball And Hole

Your opponent faces a chip from off the green. There's a puddle a short distance onto the green, between his ball and the hole. Your opponent says he should be allowed a free drop, since his shot could land in the puddle, which would drastically slow the ball's roll. Is he correct? No. If the ball is off the green and is not itself lying in casual water, there is no relief from the casual water as described. Note, however, that if the ball were on the green, with casual water between it and the hole, the player would be allowed to move the ball to the nearest point of relief from the casual water, with no penalty.

MASTER STROKES

Changing Putters During A Round

You've finished nine holes and have putted very poorly. At the turn you decide to stop by your car or locker and replace your putter with another. As you head for the 10th tee you mention that you're changing putters. Your opponent tells you that doing so would be a violation. Is he correct?

Yes, assuming you were already carrying the maximum allowable number of clubs (14). You're limited to the 14 clubs you started with, assuming none have been accidentally damaged. However, if you were carrying fewer than 14 clubs, you may add any club or clubs, as long as the total does not exceed 14 and if doing so does not delay play.

MASTER·STROKES

Ball In Burrowing Hole In Bunker

Your approach shot lands in a bunker. Upon reaching the ball, you find it deep in a hole near the lip of the bunker made by a burrowing animal (such as rabbit, mole, or gopher). You say this is an obstruction and you're allowed to take a free drop. Your opponent says you can't move the ball because it's in a hazard. Who is right?

You are. Under the rules, if the ball finds a burrow hole within a bunker, you may drop the ball at the nearest point of relief, no closer to the hole and still within the bunker, with no penalty.

MASTER·STROKES

When Storm Stops Play

You are playing in a local tournament. You have just teed off on the 18th but an electrical storm looms nearby. A horn sounds indicating that play must stop, so you begin to head toward the clubhouse. However, one of your playing partners objects, saying that you are allowed to finish the hole you have started (and in this case, complete the round). Is he correct?

No! When dangerous conditions exist (and lightning is the most dangerous), stop immediately and head for shelter. If the local committee permits, you may mark the ball's position and lift it. If this is not specifically stated, simply leave the ball and seek shelter until play is resumed.

MASTER·STROKES

Clubhead Clips Sand On Takeaway

On a shot from a greenside bunker, you address the ball with the sole of the club slightly above the sand. As you start back, however, the sole clips a raised bit of sand a few inches behind the ball. After you complete the shot, your opponent says you must take a penalty for grounding your club in the hazard. You argue that it is okay to touch the hazard once the swing has begun. Who's correct?

Your opponent is. When the ball is resting in a hazard, the club must not touch the hazard at any time prior to impact. Penalty is loss of hole in match play, two strokes in stroke play.

MASTER·STROKES

Drop Where Ball
Last Crosses Hazard

On a hole with water down the left side, your drive starts well left, over the hazard. It then slices back to the right, nearly avoiding the water, but lands a yard from the edge of the hazard. You estimate the spot at which the ball landed, then drop the ball even with this spot, within two club lengths of the hazard. Have you dropped correctly?

No! In this situation, you must drop behind the spot where the ball last crossed land before entering the hazard. Given the flight of your shot and the location of the hazard shown, this spot is much farther back toward the tee. Drop behind this spot, taking a one-stroke penalty.

MASTER STROKES

Don't Alter Ground Behind Ball

Under the rules, from tee to green you must play the ball as it lies. This means you may not improve the lie of the ball in any way. One violation amateurs often commit, particularly when the ground is soft, is to use the clubhead to push down on the earth directly behind the ball. This is in effect improving the lie as it's now easier to hit the back of the ball cleanly. The penalty for improving the lie in any way is two strokes in stroke play, loss of hole in match play. So, make it a habit to set the club very lightly behind the ball rather than pressing downward.

MASTER·STROKES

Putt Hits Flagstick On Green

You face a 30-foot putt and ask a member of your foursome to remove the flag. She does so, placing the flag eight feet beyond the hole. You hit the putt much too hard so that it rolls past the hole, hits the flag and stops. Is there any penalty, and if so, to whom?

Yes; the penalty is against you, either two strokes in stroke play or loss of hole in match play. There is no penalty to your playing partner. The moral: If someone removes the flag for you, make sure they place it far enough from the hole that there's no chance your ball will hit it.

MASTER·STROKES

Finding First Ball
After Hitting Provisional

You slice your drive into the woods. Using good etiquette, you hit a provisional ball (in case the first is lost, you will be playing this ball with a stroke-and-distance penalty). You drive the provisional down the middle, beyond your first ball. After a brief look for your first ball, you go ahead to your provisional ball and hit a shot toward the green. Just then your partner calls out, "I've got your first ball!" You identify the ball as yours, and prepare to play it. Your opponent says you can't. Who's right?

Your opponent is. According to the rules, once you have played a provisional ball from a spot that is nearer to the hole than the original ball was likely to have been, you have in effect declared the ball lost. The provisional ball is the ball in play.

MASTER·STROKES

Can You "Use" Opponent's Ball?

In a match, your putt rolls up to the hole and stops one inch away. It is positioned so that it is just to the right of the hole in relation to your opponent's line of putt. You walk up to tap it in. However, your opponent tells you to leave the ball there, figuring that if his putt just misses to the right it might carom off your ball and into the hole. Must you leave the ball next to the hole?

No! The rules state that any player may lift his or her ball if he or she decides that the ball's position might help the opposing player.

MASTER STROKES

Was Ball In Hazard?

Your shot lands short of a narrow creek but bounces just over the water. It finishes near the top of the bank, where you can hit it. As you set up, your playing partner says, "Don't ground your club—the ball's in the hazard." You say that since the ball's not in the water, you may ground your club. Who's right?

According to the rules, all ground or water within the area marked as a water hazard, is part of the hazard. The boundaries will be marked by yellow stakes. If your ball was inside a line drawn between the stakes (as is likely if it were lying near but below the top of the creek bank), it was indeed within the hazard. Don't ground your club before hitting the shot!

Don't ground club

MASTER·STROKES

What If You Break A Club?

In a competition at your club, on the ninth tee you hit a sharp hook into the trees on the left. In disgust, you smack your driver against a bench next to the tee (not very hard, you thought). But to your surprise, the clubshaft snaps just above the hosel! Can you replace the club with another driver from your locker as you head for the back nine?

According to the rules, you may not. A club damaged in the normal course of play could have been replaced; but when you break a club, whether you meant to or not, you must go without it for the remainder of the round.

MASTER·STROKES

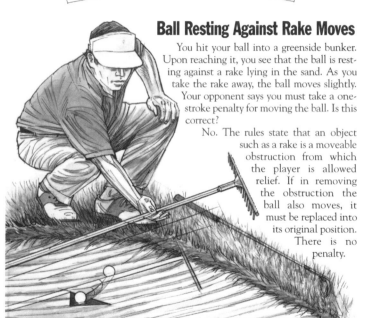

Ball Resting Against Rake Moves

You hit your ball into a greenside bunker. Upon reaching it, you see that the ball is resting against a rake lying in the sand. As you take the rake away, the ball moves slightly. Your opponent says you must take a one-stroke penalty for moving the ball. Is this correct?

No. The rules state that an object such as a rake is a moveable obstruction from which the player is allowed relief. If in removing the obstruction the ball also moves, it must be replaced into its original position. There is no penalty.

MASTER·STROKES

Ball Hits Attended Flagstick

You face a long putt. To aid depth perception, you ask a playing partner to attend the flag (meaning she should pull the flag out after you've hit the putt.) You roll it dead on line, but as your partner attempts to pull out the flag, it sticks in the cup. Your ball hits the flagstick and goes in. Is there any penalty to you?

Unfortunately, there is. Whenever a ball struck from on the green hits the flagstick, whether it's attended or not, the penalty is two strokes in stroke play, loss of hole in match play. Note: This example shows why it's a good idea for the player attending the flagstick to remove its base from the hole before the player's stroke. This way, having it stick is never a problem.

MASTER STROKES

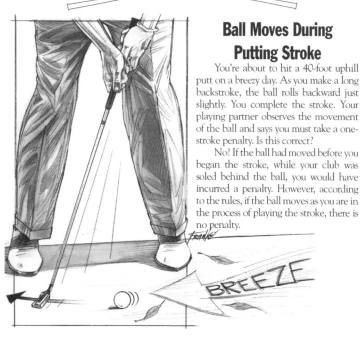

Ball Moves During Putting Stroke

You're about to hit a 40-foot uphill putt on a breezy day. As you make a long backstroke, the ball rolls backward just slightly. You complete the stroke. Your playing partner observes the movement of the ball and says you must take a one-stroke penalty. Is this correct?

No! If the ball had moved before you began the stroke, while your club was soled behind the ball, you would have incurred a penalty. However, according to the rules, if the ball moves as you are in the process of playing the stroke, there is no penalty.

BREEZE

MASTER·STROKES

Ball In Casual Water On Green

On a rainy day, your ball comes to rest on the green in a puddle. Your putt will be impossible to judge if you try to hit it from there. What can you do?

If your ball is resting in casual water on the green (or anywhere else), you're allowed to move it. Do so by determining the nearest point of relief, no closer to the hole. You may then place the ball within one club length of this point at which the casual water ends. **Note:** You may not choose to place the ball on either side of the casual water area. Go to the point of nearest relief from the original spot.

PLACE BALL

MASTER·STROKES

Two Wrongs Don't Make A Right

After a tournament round, you check your scorecard and see that your total score is correct. However, you also notice that your playing partner who kept your card reversed your scores on the 13th and 14th holes. While you made a "4" followed by a "5", he marked a 5 on the 13th and a 4 on the 14th. Since your total is correct, is it all right to turn in this card?

Absolutely not! There are two errors. If a player turns in a score on any hole that is higher (as on the 13th) the player must accept that higher score. If any hole score is lower than the player made (as was true on #14), however, the player will be disqualified. So, if you turned in this scorecard, you'd be out of the event. Remember, two wrongs on a scorecard never make a right!

MASTER·STROKES

Partner Can't Assist Shot

You and your partner are playing against two opponents. It's raining, so you have your umbrellas out. You face a six-foot putt to win the hole. Your partner holds an umbrella over you as you line up, address the ball and stroke it. You sink the putt, but your opponents claim you've breached a rule. Are they correct?

Yes! While making a stroke, you may not accept assistance or protection from the elements. It was all right for your partner to shield you as you were preparing to putt; however, she could not do so as you made the stroke. Penalty is loss of hole. (Or, in stroke play, you would be penalized two strokes.)

MASTER·STROKES

You're Late!

You've entered a tournament at a course over an hour away. Your tee time is 9:28. You think you've got time, but you make a wrong turn and are delayed in reaching the course. You rush to the tee, arriving at 9:31. The first player is preparing to tee off. You sigh with relief that you've made it. But, have you?

Not without a penalty. A player arriving at the tee within five minutes after his or her tee time will be penalized two strokes in stroke play, or will lose the first hole in match play. It could have been worse. If you'd been more than five minutes late, the penalty would have been disqualification. Moral: Always allow extra time to arrive when playing in formal competition.

MASTER·STROKES

Take Complete Relief

During a match, your shot comes to rest on a paved cart path. You plan to drop your ball at the nearest point of relief within one club length of the path, no closer to the hole. You drop the ball. However, when you take your stance and play your shot, your heel is touching the cart path. Your opponent says you lose the hole. Is he correct?

Yes! Whenever you drop your ball away from an obstruction, you must make sure both the ball and your stance are completely free from the obstruction before playing your next shot. Penalty for failure to do so is loss of hole in match play, or two strokes in stroke play.

MASTER·STROKES

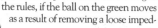

Removing Bug From Ball

On the putting green, a grasshopper hops onto your ball. You attempt to shoo it away, but in doing so, you move the ball. Your opponent claims that you automatically lose the hole. Is he correct?

No! A grasshopper or other insect falls under the category of "loose impediments." According to the rules, if the ball on the green moves as a result of removing a loose imped-

iment from on or around the ball, there is no penalty. You simply replace the ball as nearly as possible to its original position. Note: If you had moved the ball while it was lying off the green, you then would have incurred a one-stroke penalty.

MASTER·STROKES

Can You Tap In With the Toe?

In a club match, you roll your putt to within a few inches of the hole. The remaining putt is such a "sure thing" that you tap it in with the toe of your putter. Your opponent claims the hole, saying you violated a rule by not using the putterface to strike the ball. Is he correct?

No! The rules allow you to use any part of the clubhead to strike the ball. Although it's never wise to do this, there is no penalty for striking the ball with the toe of the putter.

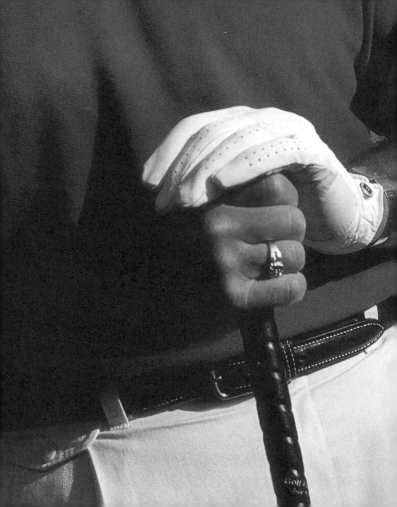

Section 15:

GOOD ETIQUETTE

If you are like many people, you may be turned off by the way the behavior of athletes in other professional or major college sports has changed. There is little or no
respect given to the opponent. Golf is possibly the one remaining sport in which the
goal is to play well and to win, while at the same time providing those you are playing with the same respectful treatment you would hope to receive yourself.

This concluding section, then, provides a number of suggestions and reminders
about how to play golf while employing good etiquette. Most of them are based on
simple common sense and a spirit of good sportsmanship. But there are also several
suggestions that many golfers have simply never thought of, that will help you to speed
play, keep the course in good repair, or otherwise make the game as enjoyable
as possible for those around you.

Section 15:

CONTENTS

MASTER·STROKES

Don't Putt Out In Partner's Line

Oftentimes you will hit your first putt from a fair distance away to within a couple feet of the hole. You may decide to go ahead and "finish out." However, in doing so, you may have to stand in the line of one or more other players waiting to putt. This is poor etiquette, as standing in another player's line might mark the putting surface and influence the roll of their putt.

Unless you're absolutely certain you're not standing in anyone's line, mark your ball and let them putt next. This will also allow you to take your time and look over the putt you have left, which is always better than rushing it.

MASTER STROKES

1

Fix Ball Marks

2

A well-struck iron shot that descends at a steep angle will usually leave an indentation or ball mark on the green. Every golfer should make it a habit to look for his or her ball mark upon arriving at the green and fix it—and maybe another one, too.

The result will be better greens to putt.

To repair a ball mark, use either a ball-mark repair tool or golf tee. Use the prongs to lift the indented part of the ball mark area slightly up; then use the prongs to pull back the small flap of turf at the other side of the ball mark (don't try to lift up this side). Finally, pat the area flat to the putting surface with the sole of your putter.

MASTER STROKES

Bring Clubs To Correct Side Of Green

Golfers need to be aware of keeping up the pace of play. Many times you'll see a player drop his or her clubs to the side of the green away from the next tee. Then, after the group has putted out, the player has to go back to the far side of the green, then cross it again while the group behind is waiting.

Whether riding in a cart or walking, and particularly if you're playing a course you're not familiar with, make it a habit to look to where the next tee is. Once you've hit to the green, bring your clubs to the side of the green nearest the next tee. You'll help keep play moving that way.

Next tee

MASTER·STROKES

Where To Stand As Player Tees Off

When you're waiting to hit while another player is teeing off, always stand to the right of and several feet behind the player, making sure you're far enough away so you are outside his/her field of vision.

By standing in this position, there's no chance of your being hit either by the player's swing or by the shot. Also, the hitter knows where you are. If you stand behind the hitter's back, he or she will be uncertain where you are and could be thinking about whether you are within reach of the swinging club. This could easily disturb the player's concentration.

MASTER·STROKES

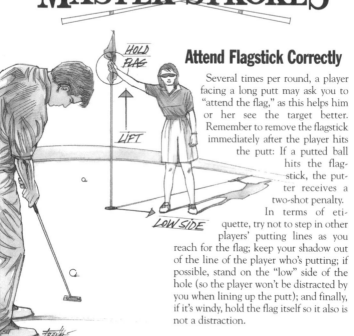

HOLD FLAG

LIFT

LOW SIDE

Attend Flagstick Correctly

Several times per round, a player facing a long putt may ask you to "attend the flag," as this helps him or her see the target better. Remember to remove the flagstick immediately after the player hits the putt: If a putted ball hits the flagstick, the putter receives a two-shot penalty.

In terms of etiquette, try not to step in other players' putting lines as you reach for the flag; keep your shadow out of the line of the player who's putting; if possible, stand on the "low" side of the hole (so the player won't be distracted by you when lining up the putt); and finally, if it's windy, hold the flag itself so it also is not a distraction.

MASTER·STROKES

Let Others Play Through

Slow play has always been one of golf's problems. A single group that takes five hours to play 18 holes dictates that it will take that long for everyone behind them, too.

If one or more players in your foursome is having trouble in the woods, and you've noticed that the group behind you is constantly waiting for you to get out of range, wave them ahead and let them play through. Letting a group through that you are slowing up is good course etiquette. Also, you'll play better if you know others aren't breathing down your neck.

MASTER·STROKES

Don't Walk Too Far Ahead

Whenever a member of your foursome is preparing to play a full shot, don't walk too far ahead of him or her. Even if you are off to the side, if you are 50 yards ahead of the player you are putting yourself in unnecessary jeopardy 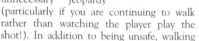 (particularly if you are continuing to walk rather than watching the player play the shot!). In addition to being unsafe, walking too far ahead is bad etiquette: The player who's hitting is likely to be distracted by you and it could affect his or her play of the shot.

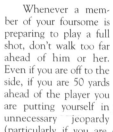

MASTER·STROKES

Keep Quiet While Others Hit

Golf is one sport in which (thankfully!) sportsmanship and etiquette are still held in high regard. An important part of good etiquette is to stay silent during the moments when an opponent is both setting up to and playing his or her shot. Any noise you make by talking can distract or unsettle a player, even if you thought you were saying something quietly and wouldn't be heard. So, refrain from speaking until everyone has hit. You'll have plenty of time to talk as you walk down the fairway.

MASTER·STROKES

Replace Your Divots

Little in golf is more frustrating than to hit a perfect drive down the fairway, only to find it has come to rest in a divot hole. The ensuing shot, if not impossible, is very difficult.

Don't be one of those golfers who simply walks away after taking a deep divot. If playing on bentgrass fairways, the divot will usually be in one piece. Retrieve it and tamp it down carefully into its original position. If you are playing from Bermuda fairways where the divot tends to "spray," don't try to replace it. Instead kick in the edges of the divot, as this aids the re-growing process (inset). On the tees of par-3 holes, fill the divot with the sand/fertilizer mixture which is often available.

MASTER·STROKES

Stay Still Until Opponent Completes Swing

One small piece of poor golf etiquette (some would call it gamesmanship) occurs when players are teeing off. If you have already hit, there is sometimes a tendency to start walking just as the last person to tee off is making his or her swing. Sometimes it's simply anxiety to get going to your next shot. But sometimes players deliberately take a step just as the player comes through impact. This movement will usually be caught by the player hitting, and it can be very disconcerting. Have the courtesy to stay still until all players have completed their swings. Only then walk briskly to your ball.

MASTER·STROKES

3

Take Three Clubs From Cart

Often when riding in a golf cart, you will be required to keep it on the path. Sometimes you'll have to park the cart well away from where your ball lies. In this situation, don't just take one club over to your ball. The shot may be longer or shorter than you thought, or the lie you have might require some club adjustment. Instead, take three clubs with you: The club you think you will need (for example, a 7-iron), and one club more and one less (a 6-iron and an 8-iron). You're pretty much assured of having the proper club with you so you needn't go all the way back to the cart, slowing play.

MASTER·STROKES

Mark Spot On Wayward Shots

Lost balls are a damaging to the scorecard and also slow down play while golfers search for their spheres. A good etiquette tip: Whether it is your own shot or that of someone else in the group, when you see an errant shot take off, watch it closely. Mark its line of descent with an object in the vicinity of where it will land—a tree, a bush, a hazard marker, or some other object. Keep that marker in mind as you start walking toward the ball. If it was someone else's shot that went off-line, mention this line to that person. This simple tactic will reduce penalties for all concerned and help keep play moving.

MASTER·STROKES

Avoid Gamesmanship On Greens

If you've played golf for long, you've run into golfers who use various ploys to rattle opponents into missing putts. Common shabby tricks include rattling keys or coins as the player prepares to putt, "accidentally" moving while in the player's field of vision, or comments such as, "I'd sure hate to see you blow this one." Don't lower yourself to the level of these golfers by trying the same type of thing. Always respect other players and let them play their own games with no interference. And when you run into someone who employs gamesmanship, remind yourself that the real reason they're trying to "psyche" you is, they lack confidence in their own ability to beat you!

MASTER·STROKES

GO

NO

Don't Practice While Others Wait

Often you'll see a golfer in the group ahead of you on the green, hitting a practice putt or two after the others have holed out. They usually do this after having missed a "real" putt, and want to try it over again if only to build a little confidence. However, it's very poor etiquette to hit practice putts when the group behind is waiting to play to the green. Remember, if you must hit a practice putt, do so only after checking to see that no one in the group behind you is ready to play to the green.

MASTER·STROKES

Avoid Far Side of Line

Your opponent is putting from about 25 feet out. You face a putt from 15 feet that's on the opposite side of the hole. As your opponent putts, you crouch well behind where your ball is marked, perhaps 50 feet from your opponent. Is there any problem with where you're located?

In terms of good playing etiquette, yes. Although you're a good distance away, you're still positioned on your opponent's line of putt, and thus in his or her line of sight. Your presence there is likely to distract the player. Make sure to move well to one side or the other, out of your opponent's direct line of sight.

MASTER·STROKES

YAK
YAK
YAK

Leave Your Cell Phone Home!

Golf is one of the few sports where consideration for your opponent is still valued. With that in mind, it's very poor etiquette to use a cell phone when playing. You shouldn't be involved in outside conversations while playing because it's easy to forget that as you're talking, a nearby player is trying to hit a shot. Second, the cell phone may "beep" at just the wrong time (for another player or maybe yourself!) Finally, you'll hurt your own game: You simply can't concentrate fully on each shot situation if you're talking on the phone (or thinking about a call). So, make it a rule to leave the cell phone home, or at least, in your car.

MASTER·STROKES

Wait Till Players Are Out of Range

Hitting into the group ahead of you is a major breach of golf etiquette as well as a major safety issue. If you have any doubt about whether the players in the group ahead of you are out of range of your shot, wait!

Most often, hitting into the group ahead occurs when you're teeing off and they're down the fairway. Sometimes it's hard to judge how far away the next group is and also, how far your drive may travel. It may go farther than normal if the wind is behind you or the fairway is hard. So, always check to make sure that all members of the group ahead are out of range, even if you hit your "Sunday best" drive.

MASTER·STROKES

Prepare While Others Hit

"166 yards... wind slightly against... green soft... 5-iron."

Slow play is one of the game's big problems. Every golfer can help speed play by being ready to go when it's their turn to hit. While waiting for your playing partners to hit, don't just talk to someone or think about things you need to do after the round. Use the time to consider your own shot. Depending on whether it's a drive, approach shot or putt, you should be thinking about the target you want to hit, the yardage, wind and ground conditions, the club you should select or the break in the green's surface. When it's your turn, you should have club in hand, a clear picture of the shot you'll play and be ready to begin your pre-shot routine.

MASTER·STROKES

Don't Play Like the Pros

Everyone wants to play as well as the pros we watch on television. However, you don't want to mimic the amount of time many of them take to play their shots. "Over-studying" the shot is the biggest reason for slow play in golf.

The pros have some excuse for analyzing shots at length. It's their livelihood, and they're playing for millions each week. You're not. Also, keep in mind that the professional hits an average of 70 shots per round, while you may play 90, 100 or more. If you spend the same amount of time per shot as they do, you might not finish before dark! So, keep it in perspective. Look over each shot, draw your conclusions on how to play it, and then step up and hit without delay.

MASTER·STROKES

Don't Write Scores While On Green

With more and more people taking up golf and courses becoming more crowded, everyone should do all they can to keep play moving. Don't ever loiter on the green of a hole you've finished, making people behind you wait while you figure out the scores for your foursome. Instead, move immediately onto the next tee before writing down your scores. You'll have plenty of time to do this while the other members of your group are preparing to hit.